ALL CORNWALL

THUNDERS AT

MY DOOR

ALL CORNWALL THUNDERS AT MY DOOR

A BIOGRAPHY OF CHARLES CAUSLEY

LAURENCE GREEN

The Cornovia Press

SHEFFIELD

Published by The Cornovia Press, Sheffield, 2013.

Extracts of poems by Charles Causley are © The Estate of Charles Causley and are used with the kind permission of David Higham Associates.

ISBN 978 1 908878 08 3

For Alice Oswald and Kevin Pyne

friends and poets

CONTENTS

Foreword

LIKE A LOT OF PEOPLE who will have purchased this fine bio-graphy, seemingly, Charles Causley has been with me all of my life. *Figgie Hobbin*, his defining and early collection of children's verse, first pub-lished in 1970, had somehow found its way into the small library at Fox-hole Primary School. Tucked away in the middle of the china clay moonscape of mid-Cornwall, its position on the book shelves there was perhaps an early epiphany of what was to follow in my own life. I must have first read the collection sometime in 1974 when I was around seven years old. The volume was, according to later jacket blurbs, 'firmly Cornish in flavour, sometimes savoury and sometimes sweet'. Such a claim might also be applied on the life of Charles Causley.

I had no idea where I was going or what I would do with my life, but I had a feeling even then, that 'My Young Man's a Cornishman', 'Ramhead and Dodman' and 'Mary, Mary Magdalene' were sending me in a certain direction. I was, of course, not the only consumer of that col-lection, for the many young readers who enjoyed its verse catapulted Causley firmly in the direction as being one of the foremost children's poets of the modern Age. Unbeknown to me then, he was also of one of the foremost poets of the twentieth century.

In my teenage years, he was there again—popping up in collections of verse read at Secondary School (these were incredible poems like 'Song of the Dying Gunner AA1' and 'Timothy Winters'), and he was al-ways a name I heard spoken of when my family took trips east to view Launceston Castle and Rough Tor: at the latter location I would hear of 'The Ballad of Charlotte Dymond'). Perhaps for a while, I forgot him, but he was soon back again ('bursting out like a jack-in-the-box'): a tutor of mine at University College Cardiff, Dr Roger Ellis, was from Australia and knew of Causley's time as writer-in-residence at the University of Western Australia. This period in Causley's life had inspired many of the poems in his 1984 collection *Secret Destinations*. Roger got me looking at these poems and encouraged me to re-visit the entire Causley canon as part of a dissertation on Anglo-Cornish Literature for my Bachelor of Arts degree in English Literature. Needless to say, I was soon writing to Causley, as well as some of his other Cornish literary contemporaries— among them Jack Clemo, A. L. Rowse and D. M. Thomas. Causley offered me generous answers to my many enthusiastic, but probably rather naïve questions about his work. In the meantime, I read everything of his I could find.

My next encounter with Charles came in 1991. It was in, of all places, Liskeard Community School, where he was completing a promotional reading of his collection of children's verse titled *The Young Man of Cury* (the first edition beautifully illustrated by Michael Foreman). Causley not only read many of these new poems, but also some old favourites. Afterwards I was able, for the first time, to meet him and talk over our correspondence of a few years before. With me, I had a heavy sports holdall, containing all my Causley volumes for him to sign. 'Good wishes' he wrote in all of them. I was at last able to meet one of my heroes. He probably sensed the awe in me.

As a young Cornish writer, trying to make my way in the world, I later tentatively sent my own early pieces of poetry to Causley for him to look over. He wrote back, expressing their potential and giving me much encouragement. I continued to send him my work and he regularly praised my efforts. The poem 'Stippy Stappy' in my 2005 collection *Assassin of Grammar*, is a tribute to his influence and interest in my work. Since those early days, I have continued to write about Cornish, Anglo-Cornish and Cornu-English Literature, and Causley is usually somewhere in the bedrock of things. He seeps through our literature, and yet as we know, he also operates on a world stage. He is one of those Cornishmen who has transcended both three-sides of ocean and a river.

Charles Causley continues to be with me. Recently, I have had the pleasure of editing a collection of his theatre works, and this has given me another chance to re-examine his work and achievement. As much as I would argue that his plays present another important side of his creativity, I still reach for his poetry and find comfort, hope and love within it. Such poems are old friends whom I never tire of greeting. Anyone reading this will know that feeling.

This brings me to the present volume. Writing the first biography of anyone is always challenging. Laurence Green has stepped up to the mark with considerable enthusiasm and sound academic enquiry. That said, the volume which follows is a very readable portrait of the poet. He has produced a most insightful look at the man which draws on hitherto unexamined diaries, letters, and notes. He has also walked the streets of Launceston and spoken to those who knew Causley through the many different phases of his life. Furthermore, he has grasped the nettles in Causley's existence and personality with considerable sensitivity and yet, also tried to unpick the important values in his world. We come to an understanding of Causley's loves and hates, his ideologies, his regrets, his failures and his successes. In the pages that follow we trace Causley through Cornwall and England, Launceston and Plymouth, home and away, war and peace, teaching and writing, drama and poetry, Celticity and community, folklore and ballad, love and death. Through Green, we come to know the man. We come to know the dramatist, the editor and the poet. Alongside this, Green helps us to unpick the language and culture of Causley's world. We come to understand Causley's life: somewhere between *zowbugs* (woodlice) and *helving* (alarmed lowing) cows, amidst *backsyvore* (back to front) *logan* (rocking) stones, Zig Zag and Sall Scratch. Quarter-Jacks merge with Obby Oss. Union Street meets Giglet's Market. In his world, dancing bears rest close to Eden Rock.

Any biographer of Causley has many challenges. Causley's life—particularly after his service during the Second World War—may seem nondescript and parochial, but as Green shows us, the poet's post-war life was far from that. In knowing more about Causley, we come to know more about the poems and plays themselves—to put it in Marxist literary terms, to understand further 'their moment of production'. As readers, we often make assumptions about those who we admire or wish to know more about. Here, we might assume Causley was a rather shy and socially incongruent young man, and yet the truth is somewhat different. Green argues for a more complex understanding of Causley which accounts for the complexity and importance of his literary achievement. The biographer shows how, for Causley, 'All Cornwall thunders at his door'. In this remarkable exploration, Green shows us Causley's incredible life, a biography built firmly 'in the sea-roads of the moor'.

Dr Alan M. Kent
Feast of St Mary Magdalene, 2012

PREFACE

Many people helped me in varying degrees to write this first biography of Mr Causley. Great thanks to Alice Oswald who encouraged me to attempt the writing of this book and has continued to encourage me at every stage, and also to Kevin Pyne whose encyclopaedic knowledge of Mr Causley and of Cornwall have proved invaluable. He and his publisher, Richard Webb, kindly gave me permission to use his fine poem 'At the Memorial Service for Charles Causley'.

I should like to thank the late Dr Alick Cameron and his wife Angela, of Trusham in Devon, who very generously lent me their research file on the Devon branch of the Causley family. Their exhaustive research included photocopies of birth and death records and records of Causleys buried in St Michael's churchyard, as well as other information without which this book could not have been written. I should like to thank Georgia Glover of David Higham Associates for sorting out the granting, for a price, of copyright permission. She answered all my awkward questions with thoroughness and grace.

I am most grateful to Arthur Wills of Launceston who was a lifelong friend and confidant of Mr Causley. In his gentle, precise way he told me a lot about what a kind and generous man Mr Causley was and gave many insights into his character and his poetry. He also very kindly supplied me with photographs of the young Causley, and of his mother. My research in Launceston began and ended with him.

Dr Michael Hanke of the University of Fulda kindly answered some important questions and gave me great encouragement.

Enormous thanks are due to Richard Graham, former owner of the Bookshop in Church Street, Launceston, who has quietly and consistently pointed me in the right direction, lending me the right books at just the right times and opening doors which might otherwise have been closed to me.

David Werran gave me valuable insights into life as a pupil of Mr Causley and Simon Parker sent me many photographs, some unpublished, with the kind permission to use them. Les and Margaret Baker were an invaluable help with photographs, information and wonderful tea and scones, as well as giving a close reading of the manuscript. Dr Malcolm Wright, Chairman of the Charles Causley Association, generously recorded over twenty hours of Causley's radio broadcasts, gave me access to his collection of Causley first editions and made the house in Cyprus Well available to me on numerous occasions. Lawrence House Museum in Launceston and Launceston Library helped me to find books that would otherwise have been difficult to find. Dr Christine Faunch and her helpful staff, especially Angela Mandrioli, at the Special Collections Library of the University of Exeter provided me with Causley's wartime diaries and extensive photograph collection, and ideal conditions under which to read and study them.

I should also like to profoundly thank Dr Alan M. Kent for much information about Causley's friends and for vital information on his plays that I would certainly have missed, as well as making me most welcome on wet days in Probus and giving me many useful books. He gave me much valuable editorial help to improve the balance of this biography. If the biography does Mr Causley justice it is mainly thanks to Alan. Dr James Whetter has given me much useful material and insights into the complex character of A. L. Rowse. Professor Charles Thomas and Bob Mann requested manuscripts of this biography to read and gave me much help and encouragement. Eric Dunsford, a Devonian, gave me some very useful information about his cousin, who was a contemporary of Mr Causley. Rosemary Summers sent me some fascinating articles on the 1933 prize giving at the recently combined Launceston College.

In Cornwall there is a network of writers, poets, playwrights and scholars, some living, some dead. They all know or knew each other and constantly interact. I have been privileged to be welcomed by them, not because of any slight aptitude for writing that I might have but because of my great interest in Charles Causley. I owe a great thank you to these fine people who hold high the flag of St Piran.

A biography is inevitably a work in progress, even when published and printed. Like any piece of research it can act as a catalyst, bringing more knowledge from diverse and unknown sources into the public domain. The whole story can never be told, even if ten years of research were to be undertaken before the last words were written. I therefore apologise for any omissions or wrong conclusions. Writing a biography always involves an element of risk; the process of ratiocination can often lead to probabilities rather than certainties. This is a large part of the thrill of writing a biography; without risk there is no gain. If I have opened a debate and raised a number of questions with this first biography of Mr Causley then I am pleased to have done so and will await the outcome with expectation.

Rather than refer the patient reader to a footnote or a note at the back of the book I will, when quoting Causley's poems, give a page and line or verse reference from the *Collected Poems 1951 – 2000* (given as *CP*) published by Macmillan. Where the poem is not included in the collection I will specify the edition and the date of publication.

Laurence Green

11th December 2011 – 1st July 2013, Ashprington, Devon

INTRODUCTION

My room is a bright glass cabin,
    All Cornwall thunders at my door,
And the white ships of winter lie
    In the sea-roads of the moor.

('The Seasons in North Cornwall,' CP, p.31 v.4.)

Were these striking lines really written by a bachelor primary school teacher from Cornwall, a shy and unassuming man who returned from wartime Royal Naval service to the small granite town of his humble birth? Of course they were!

Charles Causley, the man, the teacher, the poet, always had the capacity to surprise his readers and audiences in Cornwall, England or anywhere else in the world. Born into a strict working class background in the small north Cornish town of Launceston, Causley never forgot his origins and never pretended he was anything that he wasn't. His genius lay in being scrupulously true to himself, to Launceston, to Cornwall and to the wide world in which he lived.

Cornwall is different; lying at the south western end of Britain it is not a county, more a Celtic entity. It is surrounded by the sea on three sides and is almost an island; roughly three miles of land separate Cornwall from Devon. The River Tamar forms most of Cornwall's eastern boundary with only one tiny English incursion over the river which is reciprocated slightly further north. Causley called Cornwall 'the Granite Kingdom,' always recognising its unique qualities of geography and culture. He was probably the most Cornish of his contemporary poets, such as A. L. Rowse, Jack Clemo and W. S. Graham, because he was never self-conscious about his Cornishness. In no way inward looking he firmly saw Cornwall's value and place in the wider world.

In Cornwall, in Devon and 'up country' there are two kinds of people when it comes to Charles Causley: those who call him Mr Causley and those who call him Charles. The latter claim to have known him and the former wish that they had been granted the opportunity to have done so.

I belong to the former category. I was about to arrange a meeting with him at Kernow House, the nursing home in which he lived in old age, when he died. But I feel that, even if I had met him, he would always have remained Mr Causley. He was a very private man with much Cornish reserve as well as the capacity for deep and long friendships.

In this biography I shall refer to Mr Causley as 'Charles' until he leaves school and 'Causley' thereafter.

While not exactly enigmatic Mr Causley would always have had the capacity to astound. Being a teacher for 'thirty years in chalk Siberias' he was a performer who could put on a good show for a radio, an audience, or a friend. He quietly knew his own worth but was a genuinely modest man. When he made a friend he kept up the friendship with a fierce loyalty. He could be withdrawn and shy on occasions but always saw the world with open eyes and great enthusiasm. He needed his own space which he jealously guarded when he had found it.

He is often referred to as 'the greatest Poet Laureate we never had.' He was the first choice for the honour among many of his fellow poets following the death of his friend John Betjeman. But I wonder if Mr Causley would have been prepared to write poetry to order, to commemorate royal occasions just because he was expected to do so. He was very much his own man and would never chase honours. If they came his way he would happily accept them; he did so on a number of occasions with a sense of delight.

Make no mistake about it; Mr Causley was a poet of international reputation and a 'poet's poet.' Much of his inspiration came from in and around his home town of Launceston but to call him just a local poet would be to do him a great injustice. He was resolutely unfashionable, preferring to revive and perfect old poetic forms like the ballad rather than to experiment much in the new forms so popular in the last half of the twentieth century. He did not pursue fame and popularity; it tended to come to him where he lived. Hence the title of this biography: *All Cornwall Thunders at my Door*, taken from a line in the last verse of one of my favourite early Causley poems 'The Seasons in North Cornwall.'

According to his oldest friend, Arthur Wills of Launceston, Mr Causley would never consider writing an autobiography. Mr Causley would say to him, when the subject came up, that 'it was all in the poems.' These are poems that one returns to time and time again. They give pleasure and meaning on a first reading but release much more on further readings. What appears simple on the surface leads to profound depths of association and further meaning. Local knowledge is a great help in understanding some of his poems but never essential; his appeal is universal.

On the occasion of Mr Causley's eightieth birthday one of his closest friends, Ted Hughes, came over from north Devon to visit him. He found him surrounded by the children who often called in to see him. Mr Causley introduced Hughes to the children and told them that they were meeting the Poet Laureate, a very good poet and a much more important man than he was. One of the children, a little boy, looked long and hard at Hughes before saying: "No, he isn't." Hughes indeed told this story against himself; in the young lad's case it was a matter of 'out of the mouths of babes and sucklings.'

Causley's poetry and plays were written over a fifty year period. He can be seen as the truest and most honest voice of his generation, a poet grounded in war and in Cornwall who universalised his vision and made his town of Launceston the stage of all our doubts, fears and joys. His poems of sixty years ago are just as relevant today; his Launceston is our town, his Cornwall is our world.

Trusham

On a blustery, dripping Devon day a tall, slightly gangling man stood in the rain looking up a narrow lane at a slightly crooked chimney rising from a sloping slate roof. 'Damn!' he said to himself as his glasses misted up once again. He had come to find the house again where his father was brought up and where his grandfather was born. The drive from Cornwall had been long and tedious and the weather 'dirty,' but here he was in 'Devonshire,' the county of his father's family. It was relatively unknown to him but familiar in many ways. In a way he felt at home, although miles of tors and peat bogs separated him from Launceston, just over the Tamar in Cornwall. He could hardly remember his father, much to his regret. As the rain dripped onto his glasses from his cap and his sodden raincoat flapped at his legs he made a decision. He would walk up the lane to the house, have a quick look at it and then turn back down the hill, cross the small square by the almshouses, walk down hilly Rattle Street past some of the thatched cottages of his ancestors to the valley floor and have half a pint and a sandwich at the Cridford Inn. Veils of rain swept in from the west as he turned to walk up the lane. He anticipated the warmth of the old inn as some lines of a poem began to form in his head …

Charles Causley's story begins not in Cornwall but in an isolated village in the Teign valley a few miles south west of Exeter, the county town of neighbouring Devon. Before the Saxon invasion Devon was as Celtic as Cornwall; today very few Celtic place names remain in the county. Devon is geographically and culturally different from Cornwall and, even today, the rivalry between duchy and county can be quite acute. It was in mid-Devon that the Causley family originated and set its roots centuries before the birth of Charles Causley's father.

The little village of Trusham lies partly in a valley and partly on a steep ridge a few miles north of Chudleigh in the Teign Valley in mid-

Devon. It is still an isolated place in its green fold of hills between the piny Haldon Hills west of Exeter and the trackless wastes of Dartmoor farther to the west. Today it is a lively place shared by retired and working people who live in its ancient and modern thatched houses, cottages and bungalows. Gardens and orchards carpet the valley floor and the ridge at the top of sloping Rattle Street. The car has replaced the railway that once ran up the Teign Valley, half a mile over the ridge to the west of Trusham, from Newton Abbot to Exeter, curving north around the northern spur of Haldon.

A hundred years ago the village was much plainer and shabbier, a working community of Devonians mostly starved of education. It was pronounced 'Truss'm' then rather than the 'Trush'm'[1] of today. Opportunities for travel were provided by the army, the navy or a life in service. Most people were content to stay at home and work the land or the local quarries. Others worked at trades and crafts that had barely evolved in hundreds of years. As the Great War approached God was in His heaven, humanity knew its place in society and all was just about right with the world for most people given good health and a reasonable work ethic.

The Causley family had lived in Trusham for generations in various cottages with names like Balls Cottage, Vinnicombes, Chicks and Mount Pleasant. The surname Causley is claimed to be originally Celtic, deriving from *caslys*, meaning a headquarters or entrenchment.[2] They were working people mostly tied to the land. Some of the men were described as labourers, thatchers and market gardeners; earlier generations were farmers, a parish clerk, a teacher and a carpenter. One Victorian Causley had left the village for London, 'up country,' to settle and become a policeman; the remainder were rooted in Devon. There was a branch that had gone to Kenton, just inland from the estuary of the River Exe, to work on the estate of the Earls of Devon at Powderham Castle. One G. Causley was photographed as a choirboy at nearby Kenton Church in 1898. He was to lose a brother or cousin, Frederick G. Causley of Kenton, in the Great War as well as another cousin, R. J. Causley from Teignmouth. A later Causley finished his railway career as the last station master of Lyme Regis.

They were steady people, the Causleys, the men mainly tall and bony, who valued the continuity of their steady lives. It would be a great

1 Causley pronounced the village name Truss'm in his recorded poetry reading from Church House, Westminster, on 14th September 1979.
2 Michael Williams (ed), *Both Sides of the Tamar*, Bodmin: Bossiney Books, 1995, p.10.

mistake to say that their lives were simple. Nor were they a particularly religious family; the Church of England had mostly passed them by. It was seen as an institution for the upper classes, folk like the Stookes who had their painted wooden monuments on the wall of the pretty little church of St Michael the Archangel perched on the ridge at Trusham. The Causleys had to content themselves with family gravestones clustered in the hilltop churchyard under the shadow of St Michael's diminutive tower.

The Causleys had come to Trusham in the seventeenth century from Lord Clifford's estate, further south towards the rampart of Little Haldon. They had originally owned more land than they did at the turn of the twentieth century:

> … Causleys, they say, walked all the way
> To church over their own land. Not so today.

('Ancestors,' *CP*, p.419, v.2.)

While not exactly having come down in the world they had not advanced the family fortunes in a markedly material sense. The world was becoming more mobile and some of the family realised that they would have to move away from the village in order to advance themselves. Little did they realise how life would change for them in but a short handful of years.

In Victorian times one of the male Causleys ran a cider house, the New Inn, adjacent to the house on the ridge named 'Mount Pleasant.' Cider was popular with working people; it was cheap and potent and it eased the aches and pains of lives of hard work for little reward. The problem with cider was its acidic and corrosive nature. It was said to rot you from the socks up and was responsible for the early death of more than one countryman. The Causleys did not suffer from the ill effects of cider to a greater extent than any other Trusham family but it must have claimed a number of victims from the family.

Life was generally shorter at the turn of the twentieth century; families had many children in the knowledge that not all would survive to adulthood. Disease and accidents killed many people, young and old. It seemed that life would continue forever in a similar vein despite the changes percolating into the village from outside: the coming of the railway, the rare appearance of an early motor car, the accelerating mechanisation of farming the land. The great change that began on August 4th

1914 would tear both the village and the Causley family apart, scattering men to the far corners of the world.

Before the cataclysm erupted Trusham was just a typical Devon village in a plain, working sort of way. The church of St Michael was tucked away at the end of its lane at the highest point of the ridge at the top of the village. The centre of Trusham was a little square at the junction of five lanes situated above an orchard. From the square Rattle Street still drops straight down to the valley bottom past stone and cob cottages with ragged thatched roofs. Another lane takes an oblique and more direct path to the Cridford Inn in the valley. The inn is an ancient building, a monastic foundation, reputedly haunted, and features what is claimed to be the oldest domestic window in Devon. If you had walked down either lane you would pass cottages occupied by members of the Causley family.

The lane leading to the church ran along the ridge between gardens and orchards, with spectacular views up the valley to a wooded hill to the north and down into the valley to the east. The road in the opposite direction led uphill, past the site of the future war memorial, round a number of sharp bends and downhill to the small station of the Great Western Railway on the secondary line to Exeter.

One lane remained, the smallest and most hidden. Today it is called 'Causley Lane' and leads straight up from the square to 'Mount Pleasant,' the secretive cottage where the lane made a sharp right angle turn to follow the ridge in the direction of the church, only to peter out in fields. All that can be seen of the cottage on the corner is the porch, the door and the line of the roof with its high chimney. It was in this rented house, facing a precipitous drop into the woods and fields of the valley below the cottage, that Charles Causley's grandfather was born:

In this blown house my grandfather was born
And here his father first unshook his bones.

('Trusham,' *CP*, p.135 v.1.)

Causley's great-grandfather was Samuel Causley (1830 – 1917), born not in Trusham but in the village of Alphington just to the south of Exeter, moving to Trusham when quite small and growing up at Mount Pleasant. He became a thatcher, like his father, who was also named Samuel. Samuel junior also ran the little cider house, adjacent to the cottage, known as The New Inn and had a large family growing up around him. His wife, Elizabeth (1833 – 1912), was three years older than he. Their children were: Alice, born in 1857; Humphrey, born in 1859; Charles, born in 1861; Margaret, born in 1863; William, born in 1866, Sarah Jane, born in 1868; Elizabeth Ann, born in 1870; and Samuel, born in 1873.

Humphrey, the eldest boy, who became a dockyard worker and former army reservist, "killed himself by cutting his throat with a razor, being of unsound mind at the time" on November 19th 1917 at the age of 58.

Charles, the second eldest boy, and the poet's grandfather, was born at Mount Pleasant, but moved away from the village after leaving school to find work in Newton Abbot, the largest nearby town. He was, at various times, employed there as a tanner and later as a haulier or carter. In Newton Abbot he met and married Maria Webber, who was the same age as he. The surname Webber is common in Devon and, fittingly for a lady marrying into generations of thatchers, means 'thatcher.'

Newton Abbot lies to the south west of Trusham and Chudleigh. It was an important market and railway town with prominent engine sheds and a large Great Western Railway station on the main line from Paddington to Penzance via Plymouth. From Newton Abbot you could catch branch line trains south to Torquay, Paignton and Kingswear, or north to Moretonhampstead. It was a notable manufacturing town with rows of Victorian and Edwardian terraced houses built for the workers.

It was in one of these little brick and stone houses that Charles and Maria Causley settled down to town life. They rented a pleasant little house opposite the cricket field. Their eldest daughter, Hephzibah, was born there in 1877 at 9 Cricketfield Cottages, Newton Abbot, the family home. A change of address to 8 Elm Terrace, in the next parallel street, and the births of Maggie and Edith followed. The house was smaller and more cramped with a little back yard and with the River Lemon running in a deep channel at the end of the short street.

Charles' job at the tannery was either under threat, or his wages were becoming insufficient to support his growing family, so he, his wife Maria, and their three daughters emigrated to Canada. They settled at the town of St Thomas in the province of Ontario. St Thomas was, like Newton Abbot, a growing railway town. It was situated twenty-nine kilometres south of London, Ontario, near the northern shore of Lake Erie and was soon to become the 'Railroad Capital of Canada.' In 1886 Charles Samuel Causley, always to be known as 'Charlie,' was born, the only one of the Causley family to be born in Canada. He was baptised at the recently completed Trinity Church in St Thomas and remained Church of England for the rest of his life. Thirty-one years later he was to become the poet's father.

The Ontario winters were harsh and cold and, in 1891, the Causleys decided to return to Newton Abbot. They were able to return to their old house at 8 Elm Terrace. Charles soon found work in the town as a carter and the family settled back into life in the relatively balmy sur-roundings of south Devon. By the time Charles' younger brother Lewis was born the Causley family had moved once again to 19 Victoria Place,[3] just around the corner.

This move could well have been caused by the death, due to men-ingitis, of Hephzibah in 1892, at the young age of 15. She was attended on her deathbed by an aunt, Mary Ann Luscombe of 7 Beaumont Ter-race, Newton Abbot. Even with the support of a loving extended family the death of the eldest daughter at such a tender age must have been almost unbearable. At the age of four Charlie would have been aware of everything that was happening to his older sister in the house in which he lived in close proximity with his growing number of siblings.

In the early 1890s the Causley family took the opportunity to move back to Trusham, a village that Charlie and his brothers and sisters knew only from family visits. The Causleys probably arrived in a farm cart from Newton Abbot festooned with pots, pans and other household items. It was uphill all the way from the valley beside the rushing River Teign and many of the family must have been obliged to walk; by the time the family reached the square in Trusham they must have been red faced and exhausted from the stiff climb and the excitement. They were to live in Mount Pleasant where Charles was to work as a market gardener, probably on a flat section on top of the hill adjacent to their cottage.

Samuel and Elizabeth Causley had moved to another cottage in Trusham in 1870 and, having been good tenants, were able to pass the tenancy down a generation when Mount Pleasant became vacant. Charlie had finally come home to the village of his ancestors. He was happy to exchange the streets of Newton Abbot for the deep twisting lanes, woods and fields of Trusham. He took to country life straight away and soon forgot his former urban life, promptly acquiring a dog and supple-menting the family's diet with rabbits. He roamed the whole parish

---

3   Now demolished and replaced with a narrow park beside the River Lemon.

Grandfather Charles Causley (back row centre), Father Charlie Causley (back row left)
and family members, Trusham, 1908.

(Special Collections Library, Exeter University.)

exploring out-of-the way places but avoiding the quarries in the valley of the Teign not far from the river. Life had become sweet with the children at the village school and Causley relations all over the village.

In 1895 tragedy visited the family once again. Edith, the youngest daughter, was twelve years old with long hair and an exuberant manner. She, Maggie and Charlie were asked to deliver something to some men working in a lime kiln on Blackley Brake about a mile from their cottage. When they arrived Edith either fell into the fire in the kiln or was playing with matches. The result of this lack of attention was fatal; Edith's long hair was soon ablaze and she died of her burns. Maggie watched helplessly while Charlie tried to beat out the flames with his hands.

> The boy, my father, beating hand to bone
> On the hard flame that struck a breath away
> And turned a body and blood to a black stone.

('Dora,' *CP*, p.280, v.4.)

Once more Charlie's life was blighted by a family tragedy and once more the crushing weight of loss descended on the family who had come back to Trusham hoping for a new start.

In December 1896 a last baby daughter was born to Charles and Maria Causley at Mount Pleasant. She was named Norah, and given the second name Edith in memory of her late sister. At the time her father Charles was described as a 'general labourer'; his signature on the birth register shows a fine confidant hand. It is interesting to see that the birth was not registered until Norah was two months old. Perhaps she was a sickly child whose early chance of survival had not been high.

Life gradually returned to normal at Mount Pleasant. When each child left school at around twelve years old with their leaving certificate they had to find a job as soon as possible. Maggie, Charlie's older sister, had gone to work at a laundry in Trusham but Charlie had to look further afield for employment. He was a smart lad of average height who liked to dress well and had a certain bold style about him. Eventually he found a good job as a groom and gardener to a doctor who lived at Brimley House in Teignmouth.

Charlie left home and probably caught the train from Trusham to Newton Abbot, changing onto the main line that followed the estuary of the River Teign to its mouth at Teignmouth. It was a short journey that followed the river from the edge of Dartmoor to the point where it enters the English Channel. Teignmouth was a smart seaside resort as well as a working port where china clay was transferred from railway trucks to small coasters. Keats had spent some time there in 1818 sunning himself on the wide beach below the red sandstone cliffs where the railway was later to be built on a massive sea wall. He was there to look after his dying brother Thomas. While in Teignmouth he finished his long poem *Endymion*.

> By the wild sea-wall I wandered
>   Blinded by the salting sun
> While the sulky Channel thundered
>   Like an old Trafalgar gun.

('Keats at Teignmouth, Spring, 1818,' *CP*, p.1, v.1.)

Charlie must have been very happy working in Teignmouth, taking great pride in his work and appearance. He had a promising future and the determination to do well for himself. The years passed profitably as Charlie took on more and more responsibility. Across the Channel the clouds of war were beginning to gather as the Kaiser's Germany began to demand a dominant role in Europe. The stone cast by the late Queen Victoria's cousin in central Europe was to cast ripples that reached to the shores of the Channel and the port of Teignmouth.

In the meantime Charlie had met a charming young Cornish girl who worked in service at the house next door. Her name was Laura Jane Bartlett and she came from the little village of Langore near Launceston in north Cornwall. She pronounced the town's name 'Lanson'; her accent was slightly different to Charlie's 'cider sharp' Devonian. Charlie was two years older than Laura and they were soon walking out together.

> THEY ARE waiting for me somewhere beyond Eden Rock:
> My father, twenty-five, in the same suit
> Of Genuine Irish Tweed, his terrier Jack
> Still two years old and trembling at his feet.
>
> My mother, twenty-three, in a sprigged dress
> Drawn at the waist, ribbon in her straw hat,
> Has spread the stiff white cloth over the grass.
> Her hair, the colour of wheat, takes on the light.

('Eden Rock,' *CP*, p.421.)

Charlie and Laura Causley's wedding photograph taken in Teignmouth in February 1915.

(Special Collections Library, Exeter University.)

They became engaged and Charlie volunteered to fight with the British Army on November 11th 1914 in Torquay. He had a studio photograph taken soon afterwards in his smart new uniform with lanyard round the left shoulder and a belt of leather cartridge pouches aslant over his chest. Charlie and Laura were married on 6th February 1915 at the church of St Thomas the Apostle in Launceston, Cornwall, when Charlie was home on leave. Their wedding photograph had previously been taken in Teignmouth. Laura, as his wife, would now receive a proportion of his pay when he was on overseas service in France or Belgium but had to give up her job in service in Teignmouth. She moved back to live with her mother in Cornwall while Charlie was away at the front.

> Year of the *Lusitania*; gas
> Used at the Front; Arras and Ypres
> More than place-names. 1915.

('Wedding Portrait,' *CP*, p.271 v.1.)

Laura had brothers who had gone away from Cornwall to fight the Hun but Charlie was the only one of his family to go. He was in his late twenties and gave up a good safe job in a pleasant town to fight in disgusting conditions for King and country. He felt that he had no choice and was determined to do his duty to the country that had been good to him.

Because he had a good knowledge of horses and a good way with them Charlie Causley became a Driver in the Royal Army Service Corps attached to the Second Wessex Division. His Army number was T/344325.

> My father, Driver Causley, stands
> Speckless in 2nd Wessex kit,
> A riding-crop in ordered hands,
> Lanyard well slicked, and buttons lit
> With Brasso; military cap
> On the fake pillar for an urn
> Khaki roughens the neck.

(*ibid.*, p.271 v. 2.)

- 14 -

Charlie had a hard war. He lost his right index finger in an accident with a horse during a bombardment on the Somme and contracted tuberculosis of the lungs in the trenches as the result of a phosgene gas attack. Now, unable to fire a rifle or to tie his own bootlaces, he was invalided out of the army in 1919 after serving for four years and two hundred and twenty-eight days. He was discharged 'being surplus to military requirements having suffered impairment since entry into the service.' When he returned home his health was much diminished and he could no longer do the demanding job for which he had been taken on at Brimley House in Teignmouth. He had become bony and prematurely aged; yet another victim of the 'War to End all Wars.' He had a disability pension but the workhouse was always looming at the back of their minds. He also brought home a German *Pickelhaube*, a spiked leather German helmet, in which he had very neatly written his name in slanted pencilled capital letters, and his two campaign medals 'Mutt and Jeff.'[4]

He and Laura decided to stay in Launceston where there would be some prospect of a job and support from Laura's large family. In early 1917 Laura and Charlie were delighted to learn that they were expecting a baby. They had settled into the rented house called 'Riverside' where Laura and her mother had lived while Charlie was at the front. It sat across the road from the River Kensey, a few yards from the ancient church of St Thomas in the valley below the frowning castle ruins on the edge of Launceston, in the area known as 'St Thomas Hamlet' or Newport.

---

4   British War Medal and Victory Medal.

By St Thomas Water

Launceston is a fascinating hilltop town just to the west of the River Tamar and the border with Devon. It is the only walled town in Cornwall and its twisting streets are dominated by the grey bulk of Robert de Mortain's ruined castle on its mound. It is almost equidistant from the Channel to the south and the Atlantic to the north and lies between Dartmoor to the south east and Bodmin Moor to the west. A view from the castle's precipitous top encompasses both moors and the flatter expanse of north Devon.

'The image of a venerable slate and granite camel resting on its haunches above the Tamar, castle on one hump, parish church of St Stephen's on the other, the waters of the Kensey crawling between.' (Charles Causley, Introduction to *The Book of Launceston*, Venning, 1976.)

It is remarkable how many Launceston men made their mark in the antipodes and other more obscure parts of the Victorian world. Philip Gidley King, the second governor of New South Wales, was born in Southgate Street not far from the Southgate arch. Thomas Prockter Ching, a young ship's officer from an eminent Launceston family in Broad Street, was on the barque *Charles Eaton* when it was wrecked at the entrance to the Torres Straits and was later eaten by islanders. He was to be known for evermore as "Eton, Eaton, Eaten Ching."[5]

The future Charles Causley was to be born into a town with a strong tradition of oral history and myth. Launceston had been the county town of Cornwall until 1836; prisoners such as George Fox and Cuthbert Mayne were incarcerated in the grim castle gatehouse known as 'Doomsdale' and public executions were held on the Castle Green. Barnicoat and Thompson, robbers and murderers, died slowly on the gallows before a huge and appreciative crowd in the late 1820s.

---

5   See Laurence Green, *A Hollow Sea: Thomas Prockter Ching and the Barque 'Charles Eaton'*, Brixham: Moorhen Publishing, 2009.

Religion played a large part in the town in the early twentieth century. The name 'Launceston' is an anglicised corruption of the Cornish 'Lan Stefan,' the religious foundation of St Stephen. In the early Celtic Christian church of the Dark Ages a typical Cornish town was divided in two, usually by a river. The 'Lan,' or religious enclave, of Launceston began at St Thomas and the River Kensey and stretched uphill to the church of St Stephen on the hill facing the site of the massive castle built by Robert de Mortain, half brother to William the Conqueror.

The civil, or secular, part of the town lay uphill from the river Kensey on a plateau behind the castle mound. The local pronunciation of the town 'Lanson' reflects the Celtic origin of the name rather than its anglicised version. A later Saxon name 'Dunheved' was imposed on the town when the Cornish language began to recede to the western part of Cornwall, a process that had become almost complete only a hundred years before the birth of Charles Causley.

Such was the confusion over place names in north Cornwall that the Great Western Railway, who normally got things right, named two of their Castle Class locomotives 'Launceston Castle' and 'Lan Stephan Castle' not realising that they were one and the same place.

In 1917 Launceston was a mixture of market town and numerous local small industries, like those manufacturing straw hats. The area around St Thomas' church included the ruins of a vast priory, closed by Henry VIII at the Dissolution of the Monasteries. The ruins were overlaid by a gasworks, the railway, a few ancient cottages and the odd Victorian Terrace. The River Kensey divided itself in two around a small island with chestnut trees, across the road from the Causley's front door, where it was known as 'St Thomas Water.' A hundred yards upstream was the low mediaeval Prior's bridge which had been supplanted by a modern bridge a few yards the other side of the Causley's cottage on the road to Bude and Holsworthy. This road, St Thomas Road, was still called 'New Road' by locals from a distant memory of its construction in the 1830s.

St Thomas' church was the most ancient church in Launceston, being the only remaining part of the abbey. Up the steep hill past the castle was the imposing church of St Mary Magdalene with its unique granite exterior decorations and recumbent statue on the east wall. Further along Tower Street was the extensive Methodist church opposite the Liberal Club. Methodism had gained a great hold in Victorian Cornwall because it appealed directly to the people who had been neglected by the

Church of England all through the eighteenth century. At that time the whole of Cornwall had been a part of the diocese of Exeter for hundreds of years. Absentee rectors and vicars were common, as were parishes held in plurality. The religious needs of the working class were ignored by parsons only interested in the influential upper classes. Along came John Wesley who preached directly to the people at places like Gwennap Pit and nearby Trewint. Then the Church of England roused itself from its slumbers with the creation of the Diocese of Truro, the building of the magnificent cathedral with its Breton lantern tower and the hasty restoration of the vast majority of Cornish parish churches.

It was to a semi-rural, semi-industrial part of the town that the Causleys came in early 1917. Behind the cottage, the stable yard and the gas works was the line of the London and South Western Railway that curved away westwards towards Padstow, following the agricultural valley of the Kensey as far as the village of Egloskerry. Walking along the lane from the Causley's cottage with your back to St Thomas Road you would follow the river upstream, past St Thomas' church to Town Mills and over the railway bridge to a quiet and shaded lane that soon left the purlieus of the town for the flat fields and hanging oak woods of the Kensey Valley, past farms and the occasional quarry. The scenery must have, to some extent, reminded Charlie Causley of the more precipitous countryside around Trusham.

Laura Causley was coming home at last. She had been born in the little village of Langore, in the hills a few miles to the north west of Launceston. Her family was 'chapel,' her father was:

> Richard Bartlett, stone-cutter, quarryman;
> The Bible Christian local preacher, Sunday
> School teacher and teetotaller. Highly
> Respected, leading and intelligent
> Member of the sect.

('Richard Bartlett,' *CP*, p.279 v.1.)

He was married to Mary Jane Bartlett (nee Congdon) who was a year older than he. Laura had been born in 1887, midway between six brothers and sisters. Richard, her father, worked at a stone quarry with his older brother William who lived with his wife Grace at 40 St Stephen's Hill in Launceston. The quarry lay a short distance from the centre of Launceston beside Zig Zag, the steep winding path that led from the town on its hill down to the railway.

Early one July morning in the mid 1890s Richard Bartlett was:

About to split a stone, trying to find
A place to insert the wedge. The overhang
Shrugs off a quiet sting of slate. It nags
Three inches through the skull.

(ibid. v.2.)

By midday he was dead and lying in the dispensary while his friend Melhuish tried in vain to find the piece of slate that had killed him. After the funeral the workhouse seemed to be the only place for the widowed Mary Jane and her seven children, the youngest of whom was only three months old.

She was in her early forties and was determined to bring up her family without recourse to the poorhouse. She moved into the cottage at the side and back of 'Riverside' next door to her sister Emily and her husband Dick Bridgman, a former wheelwright turned housepainter. To make ends meet Mary Jane cleaned for neighbours, took in washing and sewed and scrimped for years. She eventually succeeded in bringing up her children who:

… safely fled like beads of mercury
Over the scattered map …

(ibid. v.3.)

Mary Jane Bartlett died in 1917 at the age of sixty four, proud of her scattered adult children, owing nobody a penny but utterly worn out. Of such stern stuff are many Cornish people made; pride and a good work ethos makes them consider the word 'dogged' to be a great compliment.

In 1917 Stanley Bartlett, Laura's younger brother, died in Prince Rupert, British Columbia. He had left Cornwall well before the war to live in Canada and work, initially as a lumberjack. In 1916 he joined the Canadian Army with a view to farming in Canada after the war. Laura briefly said goodbye to him on Teignmouth railway station when the train taking him to his ship stopped momentarily. She never saw him again; he completed basic training as a private in the 1st Canadians and then died of pneumonia in British Columbia before he had the chance to travel to France. His name is on the War Memorial plaque in St Thomas' church.

> He might have been a farmer; swallowed mud
> At Vimy, Cambrai; smiling, have rehearsed
> To us the silent history of his blood:
> But a Canadian winter got him first.

('Uncle Stan,' CP, p.282 v.6.)

He was handsome, cheerful and dashing:

> … the darling of our clan,

(ibid. v.1.)

He was much missed and no less than seven little Causleys were named after him. On August 24th 1917 his nephew Charles Stanley Causley was born in the 'sepulchre-white' house opposite the 'unsleeping stream' at St Thomas in Launceston. It was St Bartholomew's Day and the one thousand one hundred and seventeenth day of the Great War.

Charles Causley was an unusual child from the day he was born. Because of his father's failing health and his mother's struggle to support the family he was destined to remain an only child. It was obvious to all around him that he was ferociously intelligent and he developed quickly. While his mother worked hard every day, like her mother before her, his father languished and grew weaker from the onset of tuberculosis. He was given to debilitating fits of coughing that embarrassed him because they emphasised his growing weakness and dependency on his wife. He was a proud man who resented the reversal of roles; he should have been the provider and the strong one. Instead he was often confined to a chair in the kitchen by the fire and, as he grew weaker, to his bed upstairs.

In old age Charles Causley tried hard to remember him, to bring back the distant memory of his father.

My soldier-father, Devon hill-village boy,
The Doctor's sometime gardener and groom
Hunches before me on a kitchen chair
Possessed by fearful coughing. Beats the floor.

('To my Father,' CP, p.410 v.2.)

He also remembered the good times:

… He takes me to
The fair, the Plymouth pantomime, the point-
To-point …

(ibid. v.4.)

Charlie was proud of his bright young son who would read the newspaper to him at five years old. Charles was also proud of the memory of his father who he remembers as an immaculately dressed man who did what he could with his young son. In his late poems about his father he always sees him as smartly turned out, humorous and twenty-seven or twenty-five. This was an ironic observation because Charlie Causley was twenty-nine when he married and thirty-one when Charles was born. It is as if he is seen as almost perfect, entirely whole before the corrosive war service that was to radically shorten his life.

He was, however, not seen as entirely omniscient; at Tavistock Goosey Fair:

My father bought a guinea for half-a-crown
The guinea was a farthing painted gold.

('Tavistock Goose Fair,' CP, p.274 v.5.)

Charles grew up surrounded by family and friends. The Great War continued to cast its long shadow over the family but there were fields and woods to explore and stories to hear and take in. There was much about old Launceston that was both mythical and mystical. The ancient church of St Thomas cast a spell over the family; one of Laura's jobs was to bake the communion bread for the church services. Newport and St Thomas hamlet were places of smells and bells. The gas-court, as it was locally called, was a gasometer for coal gas. Small children with whooping cough were brought from all over town to smell the pungent gas which was reckoned to cure their affliction. Hender's Tannery at the far side of the river could be pungent too, as could St Thomas Water when low and sluggish in high summer.

There was no public clock in Newport and people told the time by the shift bells at the tannery and at Hoskins' Iron Foundry in Western Road. Before rain the quarterjacks high on the Town Hall tower could be clearly heard as well as the curfew bell at St Mary Magdalene, 'up town,' which was rung at eight o'clock every evening. Closer to home was the old prison bell at the National School. Young Charles knew that if he were not home by the time of the curfew bell then 'the band would play,' he would get a good telling off. So, like his future friend John Betjeman, he was 'summoned by bells' and quite surprised to find out that many people around him had never learned to tell the time.

When Charles was about a year old Laura decided that the family must move from 'Riverside.' She could just about stand the winter floods when the sleepy River Kensey would rise, cross the road and pour through the front door into the cottage. She could put up with water from Harper's Lake, the small stream that ran beside and round the back of the house, occasionally pouring in through the kitchen window. But she could not stand the large rat that she saw crouching on a beam one evening. Perhaps she imagined it jumping hungrily into Charles' pram below.

She arranged for the family to move a quarter of a mile up the hill towards the centre of town. She could well have seen the move as a slight rise in status, away from Pages Cross Workhouse below the National School in the valley which lay at the centre of the poorest quarter of town. The new house at 18 St Thomas Hill, known today as then as 'Old Hill,' was nothing fancy. It was in a tenement block of three dwellings with a further two flats over the top accessible by a narrow out-side staircase. The house consisted of two upstairs bedrooms and a front room and small scullery downstairs. The front door opened directly from the street into the room which was transformed from kitchen to parlour in the morning by a green tablecloth and a vase being added to the table. There was a view at the steeply sloping street from the front room win-dow with its groups of people climbing up towards the town centre or coming gingerly down the steep St Thomas Hill. There was a small yard with toilets and taps behind the house and a brick wall just high enough to lean on separating the house from the sloping street. The small family

Laura and a very alert Charles, 1918.

(Special Collections Library, Exeter University.)

lived happily in that house for the next ten years.

When Charles was just over one year old he was taken out in his pram by his nine year old cousin Gwennie and Bridie Wiles of:

..., 2 Gas Court Lane,
Between the tanyard and the railway line,

('Bridie Wiles,' *CP*, p.351 v.1.)

Bridie was considered:

Quite sensible despite her role
As our local madwoman
Of Chaillot,

(*ibid.* v.3.)

Between them Bridie and Gwennie managed to drop the baby Charles out of his pram onto his head.

Another thing.
It's always been a mystery to me
How you're the only one
Of our lot doing what you do.
The other day I read
That sort of thing can be set off
By a dint on the head.

(*ibid.* v.5.)

Charles did not necessarily believe that he was special or even different when he was a young lad. Like his father before him he had a positive role to play and usually did what was expected of him. Times were hard and he had learned a great deal even before he was ready to go to school. He could read by the age of five and took great pride in his Brittains' miniature metal farm animals and equipment.[6]

On a Monday Laura would collect washing from neighbouring houses in a 'flasket,' take it home to wash, dry and iron it in her small house. The scullery would be full of drying clothes and sheets for more

---

6   Now on display at the Lawrence House Museum in Launceston.

An infant Charles outside 18 St Thomas Hill *c*.1919.

(Special Collections Library, Exeter University.)

than half the week. On a Friday she would go and clean houses like 'Sal Scratch'[7] for half a crown a week. She managed the family finances very well and the threat of the Poor House just up St Thomas Road receded as time went by.

Aged nearly five, on a cold September day in 1922, Charles set out for the school on the hill for the first time. He had to leave the house, walk up the hill, turn right and walk a few yards down Wooda Road to St Thomas Road, which climbed the hill below the castle to reach the centre of town in front of the Town Hall and its black quarterjacks Tim and Tom who dutifully struck the quarter hours with their little hammers to be heard as far away as Newport on days of approaching rain. He then had to cross the road and drop down into the school yard beside the National School which was:

> … an ark of slate and granite, beached
> Between the allotments and the castle ditch.

('First Day,' CP, p.350 v.1.)

It was perched below the road with a drop into a green valley below, overlooking the Willow Gardens, inevitably known by school children as the 'Willy Gardens':

> A hundred town allotments
> Come down to Harper's Lake.
> In the Willow Gardens
> Under the castle keep
> A hundred town allotments
> Stand beside the steep.

('In the Willow Gardens,' Figgie Hobbin, p.62 v.1.)

Charles was impressed by the fact that the old bell used in the school had once been used to toll the death knell for executions carried out on the green, high on the hill below the castle ruins.

Miss Treglown, the teacher, must have been a little surprised by the talkative, short sighted little boy who came up to her desk on the first day in:

---

7   A Cornish expression for a woman cleaning her house in old clothes.

… regulation infant gear: knitted
Green jersey, cords snagged at both knees, new boots
With tags that locked my feet together.

('First Day,' *CP*, p.350. vv.2-3.)

In Charles' old classroom in the former National School there is a photograph of a bright eyed young scholar in a new serge suit, grey jacket and shorts. It is a young Charles, facing the world of school with confidence and a certain detached amusement. Not for him the second-hand cast off clothes of the poor. His mother always made sure that he had the same opportunities as his peers and that he appeared equal to the best of them.

Charles constantly asked questions and clearly had an enquiring mind. He was marked down quickly by some of his less astute comrades as a swot, a weedy boy in glasses to be picked on and bashed up. One of his early strategies must have been an assumed persona as a comedian and story teller. If he were to stand out from many of his fellows then he made sure that he stood out memorably and placated many of the bullies with his wit and humour. To an outsider he did not stand out from his fellows in an obvious way. He wore much the same type of clothes as everyone else, he spoke in the same soft north Cornish accent, he used the same words as everyone else. When asking where someone was he would have said: "Where's he to?" He would have used words such as "whisht" for 'ill' and "go scat" for disappearing or going away.

Being a single child he was unusual, rather precocious and, with his big round glasses, gave the impression of being academic. He also enjoyed the usual childish pleasures such as catching small fish in jam jars and exploring the streets and opes of the town. But as he grew up the shadow of his father's decline hung over the family. His early death was inevitable as he spent more and more time propped up in his upstairs bedroom coughing his life away.

When Charles was seven years old Charlie died. It was a dark winter evening, December 31st 1924, when the coughing finally stopped. Charles was playing a solitary game of snakes and ladders in front of the kitchen stove while his mother and his aunt kept death watch. When Charles heard his mother say that his father was now with the angels Charles replied, "Oh." The inevitable had happened and Charlie's long process of involuntary withdrawal from life was finally complete. He left a total of £135-18*s*-2*d* in effects to his family. It was certainly not a fortune and would have to be carefully managed if the family were to stay out of the workhouse. Only hard work and frugality would ensure that the family could stay in their house.

There must have been a sense of relief as well as guilt when Charlie died at the young age of thirty-eight. He could not have been easy to live with and Charles must have had less and less contact with him as he lay dying. It was only in old age that Charles would try to seek the memory of his late father and recreate the relationship that had faded back into the mists of time. As he grew older Charles would feel that, in many ways, he would become his father.

After the burial, back in St Michael's churchyard in Trusham, life continued much as before. Laura Causley continued to scrub floors, take in washing, sew and bake. She had been head of the family for some time and was determined not to let things 'go scat.' She encouraged Charles in every aspect of his education and he did not let her down. He flourished at the National School and, at the age of eleven, won a scholarship to the Horwell Grammar School.

When not at school or doing his homework Charles absorbed the rich folklore of Launceston and North Cornwall. He learned about St Mary Magdalene's Church with its unique granite decorations that covered the outside walls and surrounded the granite recumbent statue of Mary on the east wall. It was given to the church in the sixteenth cen-tury when the heir to Trecarrel Manor died suddenly at an early age.

He heard about the ghost of Dorothy Dingley that appeared to a schoolboy in a field at Botathen in the late seventeenth century. He learned of the death, by neglect or starvation, of the mistress of Dock-acre House in the early eighteenth century. He liked the idea of ghosts but did not feel that he could believe in them.

He was proud to be Cornish; although he regularly visited the great maritime city of Plymouth, he had no wish to live 'up country' or to leave his native town. His large extended family surrounded him with love and interest. His friends accompanied him on explorations of the hilltop town and surrounding countryside. Sometimes he explored alone, wandering over the fields and splashing through streams. The life of the imagination was to play an increasing part in Charles' development. Included in this growth was Charles' growing interest in the Christian faith. His father had been nominally Church of England and his mother Methodist. Charles took much from both traditions but tended to prefer the Anglican form of service. He was drawn from an early age to the little church of St Thomas that lay a few yards along the road from his house. His keen sense of mortality encompassed the churchyard with its hundreds of gravestones ancient and modern.

The house across the road from 'St Thomas Water' had been plagued with flooding from the garden and, from time to time, with infestations of the water rats that Laura particularly hated. From an early age Charles had a great respect for the dangers of water in the wrong places. His impressionable mind had probably taken in the phrase 'water on the lung' with respect to his father's condition, tuberculosis often causing a predisposition for the development of pneumonia. Water became equated with death, an unfriendly element that had no intention of becoming benign.

Winter was another of Charles' bugbears. Being a thin child he must have often felt the cold in the damp north Cornish climate. It took years for these dislikes to develop and they were always there to be set against the positive attributes of nature. Charles, like his father, was basically a countryman, an observer of the seasons and of the tiny changes in the course of the progress of the year. He was always a keen watcher who placed great importance in small things.

Although Charles lived alone with his mother her five remaining siblings lived nearby. The most alarming of her brothers was Uncle Alfred who had:

> ... the terrible temper
> Wrapped himself up in its invisible cloak
> When the mood was on him his children crept from the kitchen.
> It might have been mined. Not even the budgie spoke.

('Family Feeling,' *CP*, p.404 v.1.)

Uncle Alfred could well have been suffering from the effects of the Great War. He was reported killed in Mesopotamia in 1916 and all was quiet at home for the next three years. Then a postcard arrived from Southampton saying: "'Coming home Tuesday. Alf." Is what it said' (*ibid.* v.2.) Charles inevitably compared Uncle Alfred with his own father:

> I never knew just what it was that bugged him,
> Or what kind of love a father's love could be.
> One by one the children baled out of the homestead.
> 'You were too young when yours died,' they explained to me.

(*ibid.* v.6.)

TO THE GLORY OF GOD
AND
IN MEMORY OF

ASHPLANT. W.   DEVON REGT.
CAUSELEY. C.   R. A. S. C.
DOLBEAR. C.   DEVON REGT.
DYER. S.   DEVON REGT.
HUTCHINGS   R. F. A.

Charlie Causley's misspelled name on the Trusham War Memorial soon after completion.

(Special Collections Library, Exeter University.)

Uncle Alfred had seven children who must all have loved him. After he died and was buried in 'St Cyprian's' churchyard, the grass on his grave was kept trimmed and seven 'antimirrhinum' [sic] flowers, his favourites, were always to be seen on his grave in a stone jar.

From time to time Charles and his mother would take a train to Trusham to visit the Causley relations. In 1921 Mount Pleasant had been sold by the owner Walter Cleave, who farmed nearby, to Lewis, Maggie and Norah Causley, the surviving siblings of Charlie, for £150. This was a good piece of fortune for the family because Charles was later to inherit the property. It must have been quite a holiday for Charles and Laura to cross the Tamar and see the sea on visits to Teignmouth.

Aunt Maggie from Trusham was always Charles' favourite:

She was the one I loved the best of all.
A lifetime, and I see her clear as light:
Respectable, in tidy black, apron
In perfect place. Cheeks still a country red.

('Ancestors,' *CP*, p.416 v.3.)

She had all the virtues of Laura. She was hardworking, religious and had no self pity. Life was work and she just got on with it:

Tolled the big bell, dusted the pews,
Baked bread for the Communion services, brought warm

Water for baptisms, tamed the recalcitrant
School boiler, saw that everyone who came,
Season on season, was kept warm, kept dry.

(*ibid.* vv.4-5.)

Maggie, like her younger sister Norah and her younger brother Lewis, was unmarried. She saw the young Charles very much as his father's replacement and no doubt expected him to look after his mother for the rest of his life.

Aunt Norah was the youngest of the Trusham Causleys and always referred to by Charles for some reason as 'Dora.' She had piercing blue eyes and, like her older sister, a ferocious work ethic. She always called her nephew Charles 'Charlie' and had: 'Bullets for fingers, hair cut like a man,' ('Dora,' *CP*, p.280 v.1.) She told the story of her sister Edith's death near the lime kiln, which happened some time before she was born, and was not afraid of death, in fact she seemed to have been half in love with it. Charles must have found her rather forbidding because of her 'winter eye.'

Uncle Lewis, known to Charles as 'Silent Jack,' was another rather alarming character who took his meals alone by the fire and had been told by his sisters not to swear when Charles was present. He was a stone wall builder, among other rural trades, who seldom spoke when sober and had to be hushed by his sisters when drunk. He was a dedicated cider drinker and a rather reclusive man. If his head were full of deep thoughts they never revealed themselves to Charles or to anyone else. In Devon, as in Cornwall, he would have been described as a little 'mazed.' Causley inherited his two Great War medals with the ribbons the wrong way round.

The visits to Trusham must have been tinged with sadness and must have reminded Charles, Laura and her brother and sisters-in-law of what life could have been had Charlie still been alive. Up the hill on the way to the railway station was the new war memorial, set above a bend beside the road. It was made of stone from the ruins of an old cottage and redundant granite rollers from various farms, linked with steel cable. The misspelled name of Charlie Causley (Causeley) was inscribed on the monument by a local woman, a sad reminder of their loss. It remains the only home-made war memorial in Devon.

Back in Launceston Charles continued to read many books and was a regular visitor to the town library. The black quarterjacks Tim and Tom regularly kept the time as the castle brooded over the town. Down the hill towards the River Kensey Charles' rather solitary life continued quite happily.

Before going to Horwell School on a scholarship Charles had been bullied by a pork butcher's son:

I see him, head and shoulders over me,
Sphinx-faced, his cheeks the colour of lard, the eyes
Revolver-blue through Bunter spectacles.

('My Enemy,' *CP*, p.395 v.1.)

The larger boy would punch Charles unmercifully and make his life a misery:

'Poor little sod, his father's dead,' my enemy
Observed, discreetly thumping me again.

(*ibid.* v.2.)

There was no self pity in Causley's view of himself as a primary school boy. When he passed the scholarship exam to the Grammar School it was in the hope of getting away from unpleasant boys like the nameless pork butcher's son. His enemy also passed the exam and they entered the Grammar School together. At this point the persecution abruptly stopped, never to be resumed. His enemy was to survive the Second World War and, like Causley, become a primary school teacher:

Which one of us is which hard to define
For children in the butcher's class, and mine.

(*ibid.* v.4.)

As he flourished at Horwell School Charles continued to be fascinated by local history and legends. He was also learning to play the piano and enjoyed singing, especially folk music and ballads. Laura had saved enough to buy a second hand piano for £28 which was installed in the house. A lady was employed to come to the house once a week on Tuesdays to teach Charles his scales and was given tea and biscuits first. He had become a voracious reader; one of his favourite writers was Geoffrey Farnoll, a writer of stirring historical novels.

He developed a great feeling for language but, like all small boys, had difficulty pronouncing words that he saw but had never heard. For example, when asked the name of the steep footpath that led from the railway stations up into the town he replied: "Adjackent Rocks," not realising that the path was actually called 'Zig-Zag' and that the warning notice beside it actually said 'Beware of the possibility of the falling adjacent rocks.' Harper's Lake, the troublesome small stream that flowed beneath the kitchen window at 'Riverside' before joining the Kensey, was always known as the 'Willy Garden Stream.' St Mary Magdalene's church was always known as 'St Mary Magdaleeny,' in the same way that some Cornish people call America 'Americee.' If a small boy touched the iron bars on the leper's squint at St Thomas' the others would dance around in ghoulish glee calling out "Leopard! Leopard! You'm unclean! Leopard!"

Another grisly story that affected the young Charles was the bizarre end of his grandmother's old cat Kruger. Mary Jane was interested in two famous men. She held David Lloyd George in high esteem because he had proposed and introduced the idea of an old age pension. Unfortunately she died before she would have been entitled to claim her pension, but the thought of it ensured that she would never have to end up in the workhouse.

She hated Paulus Kruger, the Boer leader who became President of the Transvaal, and public enemy number one in Britain. Many Cornish miners had gone to South Africa to work; feelings against the Boers ran particularly high in Cornwall. She named her cat Kruger even though it was always known by the family as 'Krujer.' The cat was much loved and grew old in front of the open oven door of the kitchen range. In time he graduated to sleeping inside the oven and unfortunately one day someone inadvertently closed the door on him. Causley, a lifelong lover of cats, would have been particularly affected and saddened by the accidental loss of the old cat.

Even when the Causleys lived on St Thomas Hill the river was not far away. Charles and his friends, often accompanied by cousin Jessie, often took two jam jars down to the river to fish off the mediaeval five arched bridge for 'minjies,' or minnows. The bridge was low so they could lower a jar on a piece of string to try to catch the quick darting fish using bits of white bread for bait. Brown bread was never used because it was reserved for Sunday tea. If they caught a minjie, they would put it in the other jar and take it home at the end of the day, usually to return it to the waters of St Thomas Water after tea. Often they succeeded only in smashing the fishing jar against the abutment and had to go over the road to St Thomas' extensive churchyard to take another one from a grave. It was always a matter of pride to climb over the stone churchyard wall rather than go through the iron gate.

There was a legend that if you walked seven times round the base of a pillar from the Priory ruins that lay not far from the entrance to the church you would hear a message from beyond the grave. This always excited Charles' imagination and he considered the act a considerable risk to take. If the message was ever uttered Charles would not have heard it; his fingers by that time were firmly in his ears.

The friend who introduced Charles to the joys of singing in the church choir was John French Treloar, who lived on the road below the National School. He was: "a tall, pale, gentle-voiced, gentle-mannered boy with a sweet singing voice, was named after the famous Field-Marshal," Sir John French. He sang in the town church choir and was paid for it, with an extra shilling for a wedding or a funeral. He was an orphan who lived on bread and jam and was eternally optimistic about the future. He must have reckoned that things could not get much worse for him. Charles was impressed by his strength of character and his sense of humour.

While still at the National School Charles and John French were introduced to the English folk song, which they thoroughly appreciated and enjoyed. On Friday afternoons the Headmaster, 'Daddy' Nelson: "permanently in a pepper-and-salt suit and with a Lancastrian pepper-and-salt voice to match," a keen musician, would open the "squeaking glass screen dividing the two upper classrooms" and drag a black harmonium, "bristling with stops," into the centre of the room. Mr Nelson took the ninety pupils for music, accompanying the children through Hymns Ancient and Modern, National Songs of the British Isles and, best of all, collected volumes of folk songs. Under his stern eye no child dared to misbehave or fail to participate in the singing. Charles loved the words and the rhythms of folk songs; indeed he dates the beginning of his love of poetry to Mr Nelson's Friday afternoon folk song sessions. Conventional 'poetry' lessons left Charles unimpressed. He remembered a few fragments of poetry such as Tennyson's

The splendour falls on castle walls
And snowy summits old in story.

Charles always equated these lines to Launceston Castle, towering above the grey National School, brooding its centuries of history over the twisting streets of the town.

Another friend was Russell Uren (a Cornish language surname meaning 'bog dweller') who struck Charles as kind and who was one of the first friends to give him a book. Russell was decidedly left wing and was to become a member of the Labour Party in his staunchly Conservative town. At the age of nine Charles wrote a novel of sorts, a 'complicated novel based on Edwardian London Society' which featured a hero named Lord Hawk who 'was a disdainful-looking fellow with a thick, silky-black moustache and the sort of curved nose that for some reason I had always associated with the aristocracy.'

Charles realised that the history and geography associated with an individual poem is far less important than the interior history and geography formed in the reader's mind. Young Lochinvar coming out of the west did not make the young Charles think of the Scottish borders. To his young Cornish mind Lochinvar must have come, on his fine steed, from Penzance or even Land's End.

At Horwell School Charles tended to sink into a quiet anonymity. 'Sharp-tongued, over-talkative, totally uninterested in any manifestation of sport, it was quickly borne in on me that I was never to be a 'popular' child.' (*Causley at 70*, p.102.)

He no longer distinguished himself as he had at the National School by playing the harmonium to accompany the hymns at morning assembly. He did, however, achieve an unheard-of ten out of ten for a poem he wrote called 'The Jew' that he describes as 'faintly anti-Semitic':

Beneath yon towering palm-tree's lengthening shade,
Now as the brazen evening sun doth fade
A veritable Shylock of all Jews
Doth count his gold for fear that he might lose
One dinar of his hoarded, glittering pile,
While by him flows the muddy, sluggish Nile ...

(*ibid.*, p.103.)

This very early poem shows the beginnings of a lifelong love of Shakespeare which was to show itself in a number of later and more mature poems. Causley's use of archaic language coupled with his imaginative sense of place showed promise of better work to come. Some of his early work came seriously unstuck when Charles used words that he either misheard or did not fully understand.

O Robespierre, thou sea-green immobile,
Thy soul, deep-stained, was ice and did not feel ...

(*ibid.*, p.103.)

Charles misinterpreted the famous description of Robespierre as the 'sea-green incorruptible' with the result that he must have found it as amusing as his teacher did.

Back home in the house in St Thomas Hill Charles and his mother took a lodger, a cousin of Charles' ten years his senior who had obtained a job in the town. She introduced Charles to the two-penny library which offered such books as *Rosemary Carew* by the Anglo-Cornish writer Joseph Hocking. There was one passage in the Hocking novel that used to cause Charles to 'almost swoon with ecstasy.'

> There is a lady sweet and kind,
> Was never face so pleased my mind;
> I did but see her passing by,
> And yet I love her till I die.

(Hands to Dance and Skylark, p.180.)

'The sight of the lines of poetry, standing out on the page like a little island in a sea of prose, moved me in a strange and unfamiliar way. They sounded a chord in my being that I had not known existed, and my response to the words, as irresistibly as to some ancient and magic spell, both excited and confused me. It was, I suppose, my first real experience of poetry on my own account: the entrance to a secret world, discovered half by chance, and holding the promise of a form of words that could be more potent even than prose.' (*ibid.*, p.180.)

Other books included *The Following of the Star* by Florence A. Barclay, *The Sorrows of Satan* by Marie Corelli, and Charles' favourite, *Stella Dallas* by the American writer Olive Higgins Prouty. He repeatedly read the latter despite being forbidden to do so by his mother. It was only years later that he realised that the heroine of the book was a prostitute. These books were popular fiction available from the local circulating library and in no way literary. They could be described as 'shilling shockers.'

Then Charles discovered the poetry of the Great War. He had finally graduated on the piano from 'The Robin's Return' and was given a red-bound collection called 'Songs that Won the War.' He mastered them on the piano and was fascinated by their grim words. They connected him to his late father and led to his later fascination with Siegfried Sassoon, Robert Graves, Edmund Blunden and Wilfred Owen.

Meanwhile life continued, austere but often rewarding and fun. There were visits to the old Picture Palace in Northgate Street, 'up town', to see silent films shown by an ex-member of Fred Karno's troupe who had once performed with Stan Laurel and Charlie Chaplin. On one visit Charles was convinced that he had seen Charlie Chaplin in person outside the cinema. Why Chaplin would ever have come on a visit to

Launceston was never explained; his brilliant comic performances would always appeal to the older Causley. Charles soon wrote accounts of some of the films shown there for the local paper. There was the annual torch-lit winter carnival every autumn and the summer pilgrimage in honour of St Cuthbert Mayne who was hanged, drawn and quartered in the town square in 1577 for transferring his priestly allegiance from the upstart Anglican Church to the Roman Catholic Church and having Papal Bulls and an Agnus Dei medal in his possession, which constituted the crime of treason against the Crown. As a counterbalance there was Guy Fawkes Night on November 5th every year with terrifying fireworks (when they went off) and a huge bonfire.

Life was rich and Launceston was a very self-sufficient place, a 'slate womb.' London was a long way off by train or by road and almost an irrelevance to Charles and his friends and family. What happened 'up country' had only an indirect impact on self-sufficient and proud Cornish people who were to become even more aware of their unique heritage in the years ahead.

There was plenty in North Cornwall to nurture the life of the imagination. There was turbulent history and personal tragedies that became well known in the area. Such an event was the murder of Charlotte Dymond on the western edge of Bodmin Moor in April 1844. Charlotte was an attractive servant girl of twenty-two who was the illegitimate daughter of a Boscastle school teacher who had threatened to kill her if she ever darkened her door again. Charlotte became a servant on an isolated farm near Davidstow. She 'walked out' with an unattractive farm worker named Matthew Weekes but was increasingly attracted to Thomas Prout, a worker from a neighbouring farm.

One Sunday evening Charlotte and Matthew walked in the direction of Roughtor Ford. Matthew came home alone but Charlotte was not seen for a couple of weeks. Eventually her exsanguinated body was found in a stream; her throat had been deeply cut twice and items of her clothing were missing.

Matthew panicked and fled to Plymouth where he was arrested on the 'tilting Hoe' by Constable Bennett who spotted him there by chance. Once in jail Matthew crumbled quickly. Even though he was illiterate he signed a confession and, unable to defend himself, he was quickly convicted and hanged at the infamous Bodmin Gaol. Charles was never convinced that Matthew had committed the murder.

Charles grew up with such stories as common knowledge. He was

Laura and Charles Causley in his grammar school uniform c.1926.

much later to write a ballad on the subject of the sad fate of Charlotte Dymond. Other true accounts of local events were to influence Charles' sense of wonder and enhance his sense of belonging to the town in which he was born and was growing up. They were a large part of the background of his development as a man and, later, as a poet.

About the time that Charles started at the grammar school the family moved house again. After ten years on precipitous St Thomas Hill, a move down the slope to flatter land occurred. Laura, Charles, the young lodger and the piano all took up residence at 23 Tredydan Road, down in the Kensey valley. The house was terraced with a yard behind and a small away garden nearby. It was not prone to flooding and faced an old foundry across the road outside the front door. A little distance behind the house the metals of the Southern Railway began their curve in a cutting to follow the Kensey through wide flat fields north westwards towards their ultimate destination at Padstow on its wide estuary leading to the turbulent Atlantic. The view from the front of the house was dramatic; across the field the National School reared its slate and granite bulk above the rooftops with the slightly crooked bulk of the castle high on its mound above it. Behind the school on the old castle deer park were the hundred rising town allotments of the 'Willy Gardens.'

The move represented an improvement in housing and was a better address than Riverside or St Thomas Hill. Round the corner, not far from the side of the house, was a short terrace of houses called Treloar Terrace and then an unspoiled country lane called Underlane that led eventually to the little hamlet of Tredydan. A few yards into the lane a steep hill overhung by trees, St Catherines Hill, turned left at a right angle and led up to the other end of the town of Launceston. Charles did not walk up this lane, Catherine Hill, to the grammar school, preferring to walk to the National School and up the long hill below the castle into town every morning and home again in the late afternoon.

A few doors away, at 18 Tredydan Terrace, lived the Wills family. Arthur Wills was several years younger than Charles Causley and was captivated by his piano playing. Charles would practise the classics every day with great dedication. When Arthur was a very small boy he stood on the pavement outside the Causley house enthralled by Charles' spirited piano playing. This became a habit which eventually annoyed Arthur's mother who, like Mrs Causley, was also named Laura.

One day she took young Arthur aside and told him that it was very rude to constantly stand outside a neighbour's house and that he must not do it any more. Arthur was a good and obedient boy so he no longer stood outside the front door of 23 Tredydan Road to listen to the piano. Now he would 'crooky down' on the pavement with his back to the wall and continue to enjoy Charles' piano playing. In later life Arthur became Charles' oldest friend and a constant visitor to his house and to Kernow House until Charles died. He told me that he still misses his old friend and will continue to do so for the rest of his life.

With a determination that was to become typical, Charles became so proficient at the piano that he was much in demand at concert parties and other town musical treats. He also became very interested in the theatre and took small parts in school plays. Charles was developing into quite a seriously minded boy who kept his sense of humour and his sense of the ridiculous. He worked hard at school, developing a keen love of English and History. He struggled with mathematics and had to admit that it held no interest for him. His strong sense of duty and of doing the right thing persisted but something had to give as Charles grew into a youth.

In his mid teens Charles managed to fall out with God. He began to question his faith and decided that he was beginning to lose it. Tending to agnosticism rather than atheism, he rebelled against going to church services on a regular basis. He loved to sit in an empty church and look around; but for him even the Anglican liturgy became hard to take. He hoped that this mood of defiance would pass and, in time, it began to do so. In the meantime he would wait and see what would happen. Hymns still sometimes appealed to him and he refused to see his growing up as a crisis. Methodism offered no consolation at all; he had faint memories of a mothers' meeting in the Launceston Methodist church near St Mary Magdalene's church. Life was quite full enough without constant thoughts of the hereafter.

Life was indeed comfortable and full of purpose. Time passed, punctuated by the bells around town and the shrill whistles of green Southern Railway engines pulling their rakes of green carriages deeper into Cornwall or over the Tamar into England. Occasionally Charles was sent away by train to stay with Uncle Isaac Sleep and Aunt Nell and his twelve cousins in Plymouth. There were five girls and seven boys, a warm family whom Charles loved because they were a part of his family. Blood was always thicker than water and family love was an automatic duty. The family lived at Crownhill, on the Tavistock Road at the northern extremity of Plymouth. Uncle Isaac was groom and gardener to a large house and estate; he must, at times, have reminded Charles of his late father. Their large house faced onto some fields and, across the road, Seaton Barracks. From first light to dusk bugles sounded their imperious notes and red-faced NCOs bawled and blasphemed at clumsy recruits. Regular 'rowt' marches ended with dispirited soldiers creeping back to camp footsore and depressed. The contrast between the rousing tunes played by the bands and the demeanour of the soldiers made Charles think deeply of his readings of Seigfried Sassoon, Robert Graves, Edmund Blunden and Wilfred Owen. This brought Charles back to distant memories of his soldier father and, as a result, a deep loathing of the Army whether in time of war or in peacetime.

Back home in 'Lanson' Charles looked forward to the annual Sunday School Outing:

> It is the once-a year day
> Of the Outing
> To sand and sea.
> Breathless, we scale
> Sam Prout's aboriginal
> 'Queen of Cornubia'
> Parked between St Cyprian's
> And the conker tree.

('Sunday School Outing', *CP*, p.346 v.2.)

When Charles was at the grammar school he doubtless went on the annual Sunday School outing in a supervisory capacity. He was often filled with foreboding because of what would go wrong; he felt somehow responsible for the loss of a lady's false teeth in the surf and for the umbrella damaged by a ball. The day out was sometimes by charabanc and sometimes by train. Meals were carefully packed for the day; to buy a meal in a café was seen as an unwarranted expense. The great variable was, as usual, the weather:

> The 'Queen of Cornubia'
> Lurches uneasily into the eager,
> Quite unrelenting
> All-day rain.

(*ibid.* v.5.)

The first time that Charles ever saw the sea was at Trebarwith Strand, west of Tintagel on the north coast of Cornwall. Armed with home-made pasties, freshly cut sandwiches and a Thermos of tea Charles and his mother joined the party at Launceston Southern railway station to journey westwards to Delabole. After a straggling walk to the coast under 'slate-coloured clouds' they finally arrived at the high cliffs of Trebarwith Strand. Once on the beach Charles slipped into a stream and 'spent the rest of the day gloomily wrapped in a large towel, waiting for my clothes to dry and, possibly, the onset of double pneumonia.' (*Both Sides of the Tamar*, ed. Michael Williams, p.13.) A long walk in damp clothes uphill to Delabole station followed.

Most of the Sunday School outings were to Polzeath by means of Sam Prout's charabanc, less often to Bude. No 'boughten' meals at cafés for the frugal Cornish folk but a mountain of food was taken in case of sudden hunger pangs far from home. On one occasion the second charabanc's engine caught fire but was soon extinguished and the vehicle proceeded on its way as if nothing had happened.

At Polzeath the jovial vicar would usually fling handfuls of sweets into the air for the Sunday School children to dive and scramble for. Young Charles found this competition for sweets humiliating and would only participate in a half hearted way. He noticed that the bullies and the physically strong got most of the sweets and this fact made him think about the flawed nature of human beings. 'Here, in my nature, a seed of radicalism was sown.'

Typically, Charles was not a bold bather. He would hold hands to paddle gingerly in the Celtic Sea. More enjoyable were the walks over the fields to 'Sinking Neddy,' St Enodoc's isolated church with its slate spire and walled churchyard. The little church where, in the distant future, Charles would attend the funeral of his friend the Poet Laureate Sir John Betjeman, always enthralled him and made Charles think of Mendelssohn's Overture 'The Hebrides – Fingal's Cave.'

It was only on the return home that the slight cloud of anxiety lifted and Charles realised that he had enjoyed a good day out despite frequent bad weather. Patterns of interest had been established that were to last a lifetime: the exploration of ancient churches, observation of people of all walks of life and a feeling of responsibility for his fellow travellers.

'And, at the end of the day, there would be the sight of Launceston as we returned: its skyline a darkening cut-out of a slightly-tilted castle, the sharp pencil of the Wesleyan spire, the strong battlements on the tower of the parish church of St Mary Magdalene. When we got within the town wall, among the deep, narrow streets, we were safe again: back in the slate womb.' (*ibid.*, p.16.)

The passing of time was marked by a loudly ticking tin kitchen clock. Charles was growing into a thin, gangling youth of just over average height. He continued to work hard at school, even at the despised mathematics, to read voraciously all sorts of books and to perfect his piano playing. The town bells rang and, St Thomas's ancient bells summoned the congregations to regular services.

In 1931 the two town grammar schools, Horwell School, where Charles was a pupil, and Dunheved College, amalgamated with a set of new buildings and became Launceston College, under the tutelage of H. Spencer Toy. The college's first speech day in July 1932 was presided over by Lord Mamhead who awarded the Senior English Prize to 'C. S. Causley.' Charles was also mentioned as a member of the school orchestra in December 1932 when the college put on two performances of *Twelfth Night* at Launceston Town Hall in which Charles played a significant part.

In the summer of 1933 Charles was fifteen years old and took his School Certificate examinations at the grammar school. He had been set an essay about what he would do after leaving school. Not having given the subject much thought Charles consulted his mother who told him to put down 'solicitor's clerk' because it was a 'good job.' So Charles did so, thinking that further education was unaffordable and certainly not for him. There were no school careers advisors in those days to encourage a boy with obvious academic ability to rise higher in the world. In any case further education would have involved leaving home to go to Plymouth or even considerably further 'up country,' an idea unthinkable to Charles and his mother at the time.

It was a case of 'shadows of the prison house about the growing boy.' On one fateful July day Charles came home after taking his examinations to be told by his mother: "I've got you a job with Mr Finn the builder. In the office. Start after next week. Wages, twelve-and-six." (*Causley at 70*, p.104.) Although Charles did not protest, it was not in his nature or his upbringing, he experienced the greatest shock of his young life. He felt trapped; to him "it was the end of the world." (*ibid.*, p.104.)

He continued to live at home and settled down to a life of work, of clerical drudgery that he knew he would never enjoy. He worked steadily and gave a proportion of his wages to his mother for his keep. There was no revolt, no kicking over the traces. He wasn't a selfish man, his great sense of duty to his mother made him grateful to have a good home and a steady job. He had to do something in life and clerical work would have to do for the present.

A year or two after starting work for Mr Finn, Charles visited London for the first time. He was excited by his visit to the capital and marked the occasion by buying a red-covered copy of *The War Poems* of Seigfried Sassoon for one shilling and sixpence in the Charing Cross Road. He was developing politically; friendship with an unemployed linotype operator in Launceston who was a member of the Left Book Club introduced him to George Orwell's *The Road to Wigan Pier*. He did not neglect his reading of poetry: W. H. Auden, Stephen Spender, Cecil Day-Lewis and Louis MacNeice. He also enjoyed Christopher Isherwood's *Goodbye to Berlin*. His politics were increasingly left wing, a reaction to the limitations imposed on him by his class and upbringing. He was never to become overtly political even though his poems were often to reflect the voice of the common man.

As a counterpoint to his rather drab and uneventful life he began to write in the evenings when not playing the piano or going to the cinema. He wrote mainly short stories and plays as well as a few poems. He had always enjoyed treading the boards in amateur dramatics at school and in the town and had developed a keen sense of drama and timing.

In 1936 Charles was nineteen years old. He was delighted to receive a letter one morning at 23 Tredydan Road from Curwen that politely informed him that they had accepted his first one-act play *Runaway* for publication. He went to work with a spring in his step and never forgot the day that he was first published. *Runaway* was a short play written for radio and amateur dramatic societies. It is a comedy based on a confusion of identities and assumptions based on a man who is thought to be an escaped convict from Dartmoor Prison. Its publication was a key moment for Charles and one that he would never forget even though, in later life, he dismissed the short play as juvenilia.

In his spare time Charles was playing the piano in a local minstrel band with a number of old friends: Bernard Chapman, Brenda Poore, Vera Aynsley, Ossie Phelps, Edna May Dymond, Gwen Dymond and Billy Blythe. Billy had distinguished himself years ago by jumping into St Thomas River to rescue an infant cousin of Charles' who had fallen off the bridge into the water, bobbed downstream under the arch and was heading for the Tamar when Billy fished him dripping from the smelly waters.

At last Charles had gained some recognition for his writing. He was a published playwright and would continue to write plays for publication. As yet he had no thoughts of writing poetry but the idea of writing short stories and even a novel became increasingly attractive with the increasing confidence caused by the acceptance of his play.

Causley's New Year resolution for 1938 was to keep a diary.[8] He started his entries on January 1st in a neat but tiny hand. His early entries show an attempt at neat handwriting with the unusual feature of a diagonal line joining one word to another. As Causley relaxed into the task his hand became less angular, more rounded and the joining strokes were only used occasionally.

The diary reveals a lot about Causley's spare time and only a little about his tedious clerical job for Mr Finn the builder whose business seemed to be slowly sliding towards ruin. Causley played the piano and sang in a lot of concerts with a number of his musical friends. He also gave piano lessons, usually for £1 a session. He also went frequently to the cinema with various friends and played Lexicon. Play readings and dances occupied more of his time. His friends at the time were Tim, Russell Uren, who lived in Northgate Street and who he teased for being occasionally 'bovine,' Jean, Laurence, and a slightly older chap with a motorbike known as 'The Baron.' Although most of his close friends were male he was increasingly aware of the attractions of women. Being shy by nature he did not tend to ask girls out on a regular basis.

He took up smoking a pipe and enjoyed a pint of beer, usually in Launceston's oldest pub The Bell Inn, a few yards from the lofty tower of St Mary Magdalene's church. Only occasionally did he confess to a hangover, usually after a boisterous musical evening. He went for long walks along the Underlane, the tree shaded road that wound westwards through flat fields beside the River Kensey. Sometimes he went with his mother and, more often, with a group of friends. He liked the oak woods that crowned the hill across from the hamlet of Newmills.

An entry made in May of 1938 hints that life at home was not always harmonious:

'Mother tells me I am sarcastic, overbearing and don't converse with her and leave her on her own a great deal. So we go for a walk to try and even things up a bit.' (April '38)

Causley doubtless was quiet and withdrawn at times; he had a lot on

---

8   Causley's diaries (1938 – 1944) and (1978 – 1983) are held in the Special Collections Library of the University of Exeter.

his mind. His second play *Benedict* had to be rewritten several times before Muller accepted it for publication. Other plays such as *Children in Spain*, *The Little Crocodile* and *I Write by Night* were sent to Muller and never saw the light of publication. In March 1938 he sent a piece to fellow Cornishman Derek Tangye at *The Daily Mirror*.

During this time he could be irascible; some of his written comments were followed by such expletives as 'damn it' and 'by God, he is.' He sometimes worried about his health; the doctor told him that 'his nose is wrong.' He complained of looking pale and, in the summer of 1938, suffered excruciating toothache. In June he was afflicted by hay fever.

One Saturday in 1938 he was 'badly scared by a man with a grey face in Robins' chemists.' He found that the man was from Bertram Mills' Circus that was visiting the locality. On another Saturday night 'three hornets came into my bedroom and frightened me to death.'

Laura Causley must have been a little hard to live with at times: 'Relations at home are strained as Mother faintly disapproves of my new friends (as usual).' (May '38)

Most of the time Causley was sanguine and filtered out the boring parts of his life with his sense of humour.

'Parsons says: "Please don't burst into song, Mr Causley, when we're trying to add up a line of figures. It's a bally nuisance."

I say "Rats," but mentally.' (April. '38)

He enjoyed simple pleasures like the return of his old Swan fountain pen from 'the works.' One day he put some money on the horses:

'I back Phacko and Thankester in the Lincoln, a tanner each way. Phacko gallops home 8 to 1 and I am in five bob.' (March. '38)

Ice cream became a great 1938 summer favourite in Launceston with friends, in Plymouth on infrequent visits by train and in the dusty heat of a summer visit to London. With his keen sense of the ridiculous Causley always put his own spin on everything he observed:

'Perspiring parsons are being shown round me by a guide in Westminster Abbey.'

'Westminster Cathedral would make a lovely dance hall.' (both July '38)

Causley enjoyed his visits to Plymouth, the large naval base and first large city that a Cornishman would encounter when leaving Cornwall, frequently taking tea at Goodbody's in Tavistock Road near the Museum. But he noted that: 'I should go off my nut if I lived in Plymouth.' He was amused by the decadence of Union Street and referred to 'the questionable little shops in Union St.' With war approaching he found himself considering which of the services to go into. He noticed sailors both in Plymouth and at home. He was amused to see a friend who had gone into the Royal Navy walking around Launceston with his young brother who had been forced on him by their mother.

'I can see him now, clutching the little boy's hand and looking like murder.' (April. '38)

Causley took a great interest in children. He liked the innocence that he supposed himself to be leaving behind as he grew older. His sympathies were always with young people; Spanish refugees from the terrible civil war who were billeted in a home at Delabole. Miss Gladys Malbon persuaded him to join the Spanish Relief Committee at an evening concert at Launceston Town Hall. He was to involve himself closely with the Spanish Civil War, identifying with the Communists, seeing early on that it would lead to a greater conflict.

He was becoming increasingly left wing, having enjoyed Orwell's books: *The Road to Wigan Pier*, *Keep the Aspidistra Flying*, *The Clergyman's Daughter* and *Down and Out in London and Paris*. He was also affected by Vera Brittain's *Testament of Youth*, some of which he read on the high diving board of the swimming baths. Edmund Blunden's *Undertones of War* he found very moving. He very much enjoyed a play called *Eden End* that he described as a 'smoky, misty, lovely play.' His sympathies were always with the people and the thought of war terrified him more than hornets in his bedroom.

'There are none at peace in the last war except those who died in it.' (July '38)

Life continued much as before. Weekly visits to the cinema often brought great pleasure and sometimes not. Causley caused wholesale laughter by applauding a trailer advertising a forthcoming film after sitting through a film that he considered terrible. The radio was a great source of interest.

'I hear an old friend Alistair Cooke broadcasting on American folk. That lovely snooty voice.' (July '38)

He was measured for 'a slightly ginger Harris coat' and bought a bowl for his mother's goldfish. After that he had to think of ways to keep the cat away from the magnified image of the swimming fish. He continued to enjoy beer: 'Beer is nice out of a thin silver tankard.' He swam in the rather green water of the outdoor swimming pool near his house when the weather was warm enough. A small cloud of trouble followed him at work:

'I am mightily bored by a lecture on the mechanisation in the office and am choked off for not taking it too seriously.' (October '38)

Defiantly, he still managed to bring down the tone at work:

'At work we have gone suddenly pornographic.' (September '38)

No doubt Causley enjoyed a dirty joke as much as the next man despite describing himself as 'priggish.' He was to find much more material for coarse humour in the Navy.

More importantly for his future development he bought a sixpenny copy of William Blake's poems. The central theme of the contrast between innocence and experience was becoming established in his mind and was to be observed and developed during his service with the Royal Navy. It was to become one of the central themes of his future poetic vision. Causley had poems submitted for publication returned but was very pleased when Muller accepted *Benedict*.

He took trips with the orchestra, his friends and his mother. There were short train journeys down the Kensey valley to the next station at Egloskerry to visit and have tea with crazy Uncle Dennis. He went on the back of the Baron's motorbike to Looe and sat on the Banjo Pier. He also had his photograph taken with a girl called Jean on the rocks at Looe. Later he went to Carn Brea near Redruth to play at a concert and to Kilkhampton in the far north-east of Cornwall. His mother's health was a slight worry: 'Mother goes to bed with the shivers and a glass of whisky.'

Occasionally he went to church at St Thomas' and St Mary Magdalene's. He could not reconcile himself to Methodism:

'Chapelgoers are really heathen for they don't kneel in prayer but rest their buttocks on the seat behind. This is lazy worship, and on second thoughts I don't suppose heathens do it either and anyway who are the heathens nowadays?' (October '38)

He considered the view that the Christian faith was 'caught not taught.' Left wing politics was, to some extent, shouldering religion out of Causley's life. But he realised the need to be careful:

'Gerald Bishop and I think (over an ice cream) that if one wants to be a Communist in Launceston at least one had better be a nice pinky quiet one.' (May '38)

Causley did wear his red tie to Egloskerry on one occasion and managed to get away with it. 'I think about the Left Book Club. But can I do it?' (June '38)

Throughout the 1930s he had noted Hitler's rise to power in Germany and the slow but inevitable slide towards war. Once more clouds were gathering across the Channel while life went quietly on in Charles' small, self-contained Cornish hilltop town. Work, concert parties, trips to the swimming baths round the corner from Tredydan Road and writing in the evenings punctuated the passage of time. The open air swimming bath was only a couple of hundred yards down Under Lane from the Causley's house at the end of Tredydan Road. It was called 'Jubilee Bath,' had been opened in 1897 and was enclosed by a high stone wall. Swimming races had been held there under the direction of a Mr C. Lyon for years. The irony of that gentleman's name was certainly not lost on Causley. Indeed, as he used to write articles for the local papers, it is quite possible that Mr Lyon was a sneaky invention that most people would have missed when hurriedly reading the article.

Charles knew that war was coming and reminded himself that he would never let himself be drafted into the army.

'Hitler speaks and the war seems to be here.' (August '38)

'We go to bed with troop trains in our ears.' (September '38)

When Prime Minister Chamberlain agreed with Hitler on 'peace in our time' most British people, including Causley, heaved a sigh of temporary relief. However Chamberlain's upraised umbrella was no shield against the ruthless will of the Führer and the slide towards the inevitability of war began. There was to be no peace in his time and Causley was ready to serve his King and country in some capacity that did not involve his service in the Poor Bloody Infantry. In the meantime his favourite month of the year, October, had arrived in its autumnal glory. 'I love this clean month.'

After learning the clerical ropes with Mr Finn he moved to an altogether larger concern, the Electricity Board. He wrote more one-act plays and his second play *The Conquering Hero* was also accepted by Curwen in 1937 for publication in Britain and by Schirmer for publication in New York. In 1938 his third play *Benedict* was published by Muller in London. But his play *Children from Spain* was never to see the light of day. One of his friends told Causley that there was too much swearing in it. However Causley countered with: '*The Aspidistra* is beautifully vulgar.'

There are small hints in Causley's early plays of an adventurous and original use of language. Each play has a good pace and unity of time, place and action. Designed to be read or performed by small dramatic groups, they are mainly set in London and have a universal appeal. There are a small number of characters and plots that depend on the outside intervention of a stranger who is not always a stranger to resolve the story.

There are a few delightful unconscious Cornish touches in the plays. In his third play *Benedict* Mrs Carroll, described in the introduction as a 'short, gaspy little woman,' says: "Shall I put on the electric? You can hardly see." This phrase sounds much more natural coming out of the mouth of a Cornish 'Sal Scratch' than a London lady in her front room.

In 1939 *Benedict* was performed on BBC Western Region, produced by Michael Goodwin with the parts read by Michael Holloway, Sylvia Parker, Dennis Anderson, Phyllis Smale and Hedley Goodall. The piece opened with Benedict, the mad protagonist, playing No.14 of Mendelssohn's 'Songs Without Words,' a firm favourite of Causley's.

It is obvious that the piano playing protagonists of Causley's plays are versions of himself. In *The Conquering Hero* the youth learning the piano works as a clerk. He is seen as a comically unfulfilled character, a humorous version of the young Causley, a self-confessed observer rather than a doer. The rather fantastic and very amusing plot of the play depends on a coincidence followed by a genuine piece of heroism on the part of the youth's father. This man, Mr Robinson, goes on a detour on his way home from the office in order to see the King of the Belgians on an official visit to London. A foreign man standing next to Mr Robinson pulls a pistol out of his pocket and points at the king while the latter struggles hard to pull his pipe out of his pocket and inadvertently jerks the assassin's pistol away from its careful aim. The assassin is arrested and taken away by the police and Mr Robinson, apparently not having given his name to the police or press, makes his way home. He arrives to find his family huddled round the radio agog at the news of the failed assassination.

Mr Robinson explains what has happened and reveals that he is not really a hero and then a second assassin bounds into the family home with a pistol in his hand. Instead of shooting Mr Robinson, who he assumes knows his identity, he explains why he has to kill him. The police burst in on the scene and arrest the man and it is explained that they were set up to follow Mr Robinson and the assassin home. So Mr Robinson is revealed as a hero after all and recognised as such by his adoring family.

The rapid changes of attitude and the quick pace of the play make it good theatre. It just doesn't have time to creak. This contraction is typical of Causley's later poetry; it has a leanness that leaves one thinking about what has just happened, a spareness that results from an economy of language and a lack of repetition. Causley's early plays show a mastery of facts and character and of dialogue in particular that lays a foundation to his more mature poetry.

Writing plays can be seen as an escape from a rather dull life. It is obvious that Causley was unfulfilled as a clerk. A snapshot of his busy life combines his work and his busy musical activities:

'On through headaching sea of figures to 10 o'clock, then, unshaven and unchanged, I go to the Town Hall and play for B[illy] again.' (November '38)

Causley tried to make the best of his dull job and his attitude towards it varied by the month:

'I am happier at work now than ever I am likely to be. This is both horrifying and heartening.' (December '38)

'Work is easy, dull, boring. Leisure difficult and worrying but infinitely enjoyable.' (February '39)

His social life, musical performances, play readings and frequent visits to the cinema continued at a frantic pace often, no doubt, to his mother's annoyance. The spectre of war loomed ever large with articles and lectures about Hitler's growing excesses:

'The story about the Nazi concentration camp in RD [Readers' Digest] is horrifying.'

'The Left Book [Club] is on Czechoslovakia. The talk is of terrible persecutions of the Jews because of the assassination in Paris.' (both November '38)

There are signs in late 1938 of a partial and conditional return to the Anglican Church. His growing pacifism drove him to volunteer for various church-centred activities.

'With Russell to various vicarages, where I deliver notices in the wild rainy dark and flapping trees, about the Peace service.' (November '38)

He noticed a growing militancy in his mother: 'Mother curses the people who won't buy poppies.' (November '38)

On a lighter note he began to despair of British films observing that 'they really can't make films in England.' He talked at length to a friend, Arthur Venning, 'about films and Mohicans' (a series at the cinema enjoyed by Causley and his friends) and remarked that 'Ginger and I see the appalling *Last Chance* about synthetic convict.' His views on bad films were often vociferous:

'Mrs Kingdom says that if we don't greet the bad films quietly we shall be ejected by the Police not so quietly.' (January '39)

As the cold, wet winter of 1938 turned into 1939 Causley's diary refers increasingly to various young ladies in whom he was beginning to show a serious interest. He was shy and impecunious and often felt that he was under his mother's critical gaze. Unfortunately his relationship with a young lady named Jean was handicapped by his lack of funds:

'I can't take Jean to the pictures because I've only 1/9d when the Left Book [Club] is paid for.' (November '38)

'Chips and no money worries me.' (December '38)

There is a snapshot of Causley and Jean cuddling on a rock at Looe taken in 1937 or 1938. Jean very soon moved to Devon and it seems that the romance was doomed almost from the start:

'Jean writes and says I am rude and sarcastic.'

'Ring up Jean and say Merry Christmas and instantly regret it.' (both December '38)

Jean did, however, send Causley a photograph of herself on the seafront at Paignton. Later there was Joan but their relationship was also destined to be nipped in the bud:

'Joan B. says no and I am foolishly sad.' (August '39)

Somewhat wistfully Causley remarked:

'Wendy Hardy from Looe leaves the office and comes and says goodbye in a little green dress with Dutch people on it. This is a girl I like very much (but she is engaged to Paul.)' (September '39)

Meanwhile there was the solace offered by various pubs when funds allowed:

'In the pub (The Bell) Frankie has a port and lemon which almost breaks me. I stick to beer.' (December '38)

Not all pubs measured up:

'The beer at The Blue Lion at Lewdown [in Devon] is perfectly awful and the landlord criminal looking.' (February '39)

Causley hated his temporary penury:

'I have no money and mother has to wait for dance jobs before I can give her either Xmas or birthday presents. Shame!' (December '38)

His mother's birthday was December 18th 1938 and he did what he could to help her to celebrate it:

'Because Mother is 51 I arise and get tea and use sour cream for milk.'

A year later Causley's financial state had improved:

'Mother has a birthday that I arrive home in the cold with tulips and carnations. Also sent a Mickey Mouse card, 10/-, and one with a cat on.' (December '39)

In the meantime what Causley and all his friends and family had been dreading finally came about. On 3rd September 1939, the 13th Sunday after Trinity:

'At 10 the wireless says we are to stand for an important announcement. This sickens me and I can eat no breakfast. At 11.15 the PM speaks that a state of war exists between this country and Germany.' (September '39)

The immediate result of the forthcoming war was a state of suspended animation:

'Our 2 child refugees are coming & then they aren't. In the morning I walk up with the Territorials who are to [sic] Tregantle Fort. The policeman wears a tin helmet. We hear various heart stopping rumours: Chatham bombed, we have advanced 2 miles into Germany, etc.' (September '39)

Life soon began to return to a semblance of normality with Causley now playing the organ at St Mary Magdalene's and St Stephen's on the hill to the west.

'It is funny, we are brighter and settling down to horror quite nicely.' (October '39)

In the winter of 1939 Causley was heavily involved in the writing and direction of a nativity play at St Stephen's that involved a lot of elaborate scenery and musical arrangements. This play was very important in Causley's development as a playwright and poet. For the first time he had the experience of directing a play with real people. In his nativity play we can trace influences from the mediaeval Cornish mystery plays the *Ordinalia* which were performed not in churches but in the open air in circular turf amphitheatres or 'playing places' called *plen an gwarry* in the Cornish language. After Christmas it was only a matter of time before the inevitable call up came.

He could see that war with Germany was rapidly approaching and that, at some point, he was destined to play some sort of a part in it. His horror of the army stemmed from what had happened to his father and by what he had observed of army life at Crownhill in Plymouth on visits to his relatives there. He had also read a lot of the poems written during the Great War. The Royal Air Force was out of the question temperamentally and physically; Causley had read parts of T. E. Lawrence's revealing book *The Mint*. A young man with poor eyesight and large glasses would not have done much except maintain aeroplanes and Causley knew his limitations. He was no mechanic and no mathematician.

From his reading of one of his favourite poets W. H. Auden Causley had seen the approach of war. Causley's rather pessimistic nature saw through appeasement; he was to remember Auden's lines for the rest of his life:

> O what is that sound which so thrills the ear
>   Down in the valley drumming, drumming?
> Only the scarlet soldiers, dear,
>   The soldiers coming.

('O What is That Sound?')

Auden had spent time in Berlin in the 1930s and was an unwilling observer of the rise of fascism in impoverished Germany. Although his poem refers to the aftermath of the Battle of Culloden in 1746 the message of the approaching cataclysm is starkly clear. Auden used the old ballad form very effectively with its dialogues and questions and answer; his influence on the young Causley cannot be overstated. There were to be reflections of Auden in Causley's ballads and children's poems.

Caught between the Devil and the deep blue sea Causley chose the Royal Navy. He had heard that there was a trade called a 'writer' in the Navy and thought that the description could fit him better than any other. His first step would not be unfamiliar to a Cornishman; the great naval base of Plymouth lay just twenty-two miles to the south of Launceston. Despite his childhood fear and loathing of the deep blue sea he determined that the Navy was the service for him. Rather than postpone the inevitable he determined to join up sooner rather than later. He had no girlfriend to delay his departure and no great prospects of finding one at home. Now was his chance to live independently of his mother and strike out on his own at last. Like his father before him he did not wait for long after war was declared on Germany on September 3rd 1939 to sign up.

A Life on the Blue

In early December 1939, soon after the sinking by enemy action of HMS 'Royal Oak,' Causley registered at Launceston Labour Exchange for the draft. He chose the Royal Navy and was pleased to hear that only three other Launceston men had chosen to join the Senior Service.

'I distinguish myself at the registration (on Sat.) by losing my umbrella.' (December '39)

He went home expecting to be called up immediately for basic training and posting abroad. Early in the New Year he was summoned to the Museum and Art Gallery in Plymouth for his physical examination.

'Now the 23 to 28 class is being called up the 23-28 leerers and sniggerers when the other classes went are noticeably silent.' (January '40)

Causley prepared carefully for his medical examination:

'I shave furiously and wash and polish and cut nails.' (January '40)

Having arrived by train in Plymouth he walked to the Museum in Tavistock Road where he sat, in trousers and unlaced shoes, next to a copy of a classical discus thrower waiting for various doctors to examine various parts of his body. He saw men with what he considered a much better physique than himself rejected and sent back with a mixture of failure and relief on their faces. He hoped that he too might not make the grade but was told that, apart from defective vision, he was fine. A friend told him that he would be sent to the Home Fleet because of his eyesight and he believed him to the extent of sending a telegram home telling this misinformation to his mother. Such was the trauma of the medical examination that Causley went out of the Museum in Tavistock Road and ordered two boiled eggs, food that he normally hated, at Goodbody's café. He found himself all in a stew when he saw on his acceptance card that he was fit for service in the Royal Navy and the Royal Marines. The thought of amphibious landings put the fear of God into him! Back home he had a little time to get used to the idea that he had been accepted into the Royal Navy.

'So on Sunday all day I say 'I am a sailor.'' (February '40)

'I worry a little about my mother but she recovers gigantically well.' (January '40)

He went back to his clerical job for the local electricity company in the office over the showroom. His life continued much as before for months on end. Winter turned into spring and Causley half hoped that he had been forgotten, that his 'papers had slipped inadvertently through some hole in the administrative system.' (March '40)

In March of 1940 he had a strange dream that showed his anxiety about the future:

'An extraordinary clear dream of Gerald wearing a sailor's uniform under his coat and scarf.'

During the same month another friend, Ronald H., came home to Launceston on leave.

' … home on leave from Scotland much changed, quieter, hands trembling. 'I was in the engine room of the Forth next to the Mohawk when it was bombed – I wish I never joined the bloody navy.' As I write I can remember playing Red Sails for him and Daniel at S[outh] Pether-win concert just before he went in the airforce, in about 1935?' (March '40)

At about the same time the first civilian casualties from Cornwall were reported in the *Western Morning News*, the main regional newspaper. Guy Golding, aged 42, his son Barry, aged seven, and a visitor, Christine Avery, aged four, were all killed by a German bomb in Callington, a town a few miles south of Launceston. A folded newspaper article describing this tragedy is in a pocket in Causley's 1940 diary.

About six months after his draft registration, at the terrible time of Dunkirk, he looked out of the office window to see his mother waving a brown envelope at him from the street below. "It's come," she called out to him. The following Wednesday Causley set off from the railway sta-tion with twelve other Launceston men bound for various services and destinations. He found that a friend named Eric Sullock was also heading for naval training at HMS Royal Arthur, a shore establishment in Skeg-ness in Lincolnshire. All thirteen recruits bundled into a single compart-ment and Causley left Cornwall for the longest journey of his life so far.

'Leave house at 8.22, and mother weeping a little. On the station are 9 boys: Dick Martin, Bob Prout, Pugh, Eric [Sullock], Reed, Folley, Bert Furze, R Daws, Cardew.' (January '40)

HMS Royal Arthur turned out to be a commandeered Butlin's Holiday Camp with more of the atmosphere of Disney than of Devonport. For weeks the new sailors trained in their civilian clothes long after more recent drafts were kitted out with their uniforms. Causley trained hard in his tweed jacket and flannel trousers badly stained by a cup of 'kye,' or cocoa, which he had dropped on his first evening on the base. The lack of uniform was a bit of a mystery at the time; it was later revealed that Causley's draft, comprising mainly clerks and teachers, were to become 'coders' a new and mysterious branch of the service rather than 'writers.' A badge had to be designed for them and a form of uniform agreed.

'Terrible smashing sinking of the heart when we are not writers but coders.' (January '40)

'Writers' were naval clerks and administrators, their status reflected by their 'fore-and-aft rig: uniforms of civilian cut, with double-breasted jackets, white collars, black ties and peaked caps.' As a 'coder' Causley and his draft wore the 'square-rig': 'with its round cap, jumper, white flannel or shirt, jean collar and bell-bottomed trousers.' Later the new red badge was issued to be sewn on the right sleeve. It consisted of two crossed flags with a small 'c' underneath. 'Exactly what the small 'c' stood for was the subject of a great deal of comment from my companions for the remainder of the Second World War.' Sailors being habitually foul mouthed it is better that the 'c' word be left in the realms of speculation!

As a keen observer of his fellow man Causley took an enormous delight in some of the strange characters who been washed up at HMS Royal Arthur by the vast and random tides of His Majesty's Navy. 'Antediluvian' Chief Petty Officers with no sense of humour or of irony ruled his days and the snores, whistles and farts of sleeping seamen his nights. He hated the noise in the mess deck, as the dining hall was called, but enjoyed the greasy ballet of helping in the kitchens and of serving food to his mates.

'We are ready before the class comes and serve ourselves 2 helpings.' (January '40)

Before long he realised fully that he was not going to enjoy life as a sailor but was determined to make the most of it.

'Carrying kit to the Chalet is 300 yards of murder.'

'Up at 5.45am. Ashore at 4.15pm (after terrifying inspection).' (both January '40)

He placed himself firmly among the majority of men who were not suited to service life but continued to try hard at his training. He hated Physical Education and, despite repeated attempts, was incapable of hauling himself up a rope by his arms. He was told by an exasperated P.E. instructor: "You must have been on leaf [leave] when all the muscles were issued!"

Causley loved the rousing martial music produced by the band. While realising how dangerous such music was in rousing the aggressive spirits of the fighting man he still loved to hear the stirring music of marches such as the American march written by John Phillip Sousa commonly referred to as: "Have you ever caught your bollocks in a rat trap" which continued in the mind of the common matelot: " … in a rat trap, or on a nail?" He observed with pleasure the concentration of the boy who played the cymbals when he was required to clash together his brazen instruments.

He also found naval terms, and particularly the slang, amusing, aware that some of the terms had come down the centuries unchanged from the navy of Queen Elizabeth. Why, for instance, was a miserable messmate referred to as a 'Torpoint chicken'? Naval language was always to be a fascination to Causley's musical ear; he was to use it extensively in many of his early poems.

Causley found the occasional air raid alarming:

'Air raid: 10 to 1 (in the morning) siren roars and wails and we rush barefoot out onto the moonlit cold concrete to various wrong shelters. I am in pyjamas, overcoat, gas mask and later boots.' (June '40)

Soon even the air raids became routine:

'Air raid 11.30 – 4.30 and sleep well in shelter.'

'The shelter seems full of stokers, swearing, farting Cockneys.' (both June '40)

An escape from the horrors of naval life was a trip off the base to have a kip wrapped in a blanket on the beach. It is strange how all soldiers, sailors and airmen crave sleep as an escape and a refreshment. One afternoon Causley and his friend Rattler Morgan were sound asleep on the beach at Skegness wrapped in purple blankets when they were woken by a child's piping voice shouting: "Look! Two sailors asleep!" It took some time before Causley realised that he was actually one of the sailors. 'Rattler' Morgan was probably given his nickname by Causley who, with his love of English folk songs, associated him with 'Morgan Rattler.'

Naval life was taking its toll on Causley: 'Tired and depressed all day.' (June '40)

He had his first letter from his mother who told him that the BBC had rejected his play *The Frontier*. He caught a cold and spent a few miserable days in the sick bay. Then he was back in his chalet that stank of sewage and back to training:

'PT, piling arms, splicing (oh!!!)'

'We slope arms and wear fingers out slapping the rifles, Fred Karno kit inspection and boat drill.' (both June '40)

There were still small pleasures that made life bearable:

'Every day we buy chocolate to eat.' (June '40)

'A pleasing thing at the camp is to find a lavatory that has a bolt on the door.' (July '40)

After a few months of training Causley qualified for a weekend leave:

'Ticket for home is 49/2*d* (5*d* more than Plymouth)' (July '40)

He set off for his brief respite from the Navy:

'Plymouth at 7.10, Lanson 9.33 where Mother is waiting in the heavy black Saturday gloom.'

Once home he was the centre of attention:

'Everyone says I am taller, better looking (I mean healthier).'

Soon enough it was back to Skegness for Morse code, Divisions and coding practice. (both July '40)

'The epilogue every day is the melancholy cleaning of damp boots.' (July '40)

At the end of the course were the dreaded coding exams:

' … dreadful practical coding, and my heart thumps horribly.' (July '40)

He passed both sets of exams and passed out at last as Ordinary Seaman.

In August 1940 Causley was sent back to the Royal Naval Barracks at Devonport in Plymouth, known universally by sailors of the Royal Navy as 'Guz.' Although he was less than twenty-five miles away from home he was trapped in an alien world. It was:

' … unmitigated hell. Its solid, granite appearance reminded me of the jail at Princetown, on Dartmoor, built originally to accommodate French prisoners during the Napoleonic Wars. It smelt of pusser's soap,[9] salt water, Diesel oil, Jeyes Fluid, and crime.' (August '40)

The worst part was waking up in the morning:

---

9 'Pusser's' is Royal Naval slang for 'purser's,' *i.e.* anything issued and signed for. The word is pronounced like the oozing yellow matter rather than the fluffy feline.

'We are not allowed to keep private diaries. So I must confine myself to the effects of this life on my mind, to write mentally. I am acutely miserable here and actual suicide seems practicable when I wake up uncomfortably at 6 in the morning in the burning electric light and roar of the ventilator.' (August '40)

At this point in the diary Causley's handwriting loses its elegant points and connecting strokes. It becomes untidy and rounded with the occasional smudge and blot caused possibly by the odd tear. All was not lost; Causley soon bounced back to his former resilient self as he was to do repeatedly during the course of the next five wartime years.

'Ashore with 'The Things,' walking coolly on the Hoe with Wiggy, Ralph, Tom, Jimmy and Bob I am happy and in the cool shining pub.' (August '40)

At first it was a struggle just getting meals in the dining hall. Ferocious Chief Petty Officers monitored every move and pounced on any weakness or insecurity.

> His barefoot, coal-burning soul
> Expands, puffs like a toad, in the convict air
> Of the Royal Naval Barracks at Devonport.

> ('Chief Petty Officer,' *CP*, p.14 v.1.)

Another problem was making sure that all the kit so carefully signed for remained in one's possession. The barracks was crowded and everything signed for had to be paid for if lost or stolen. To the 'prehistoric eye' of a Chief Petty Officer, stolen invariably meant lost by carelessness or negligence. Causley and his mates looked out for each other in order to minimise the losses of His Majesty's valuable stores. Friends became very important in the struggle for survival in the process of becoming a sailor.

Rattler Morgan was to die in action when HMS Cabbala was sunk by enemy action. Causley's later poem remembering him ('Rattler Morgan,' *CP*, p.18.) is reminiscent of 'Full Fathoms Five' in Shakespeare's last play *The Tempest*. Causley was very fond of Shakespeare and often carried one of his plays in his pocket.

Young Eric Sullock, the Launceston man who travelled to HMS Royal Arthur with Causley, was also soon to disappear. He was 'a large, resilient youth, immensely affable and kind.' Causley only saw him three times at HMS Royal Arthur before he vanished into the vast maw of the

Navy and was later killed on near the Canary Islands on HMS Bredon. When he heard the sad news Causley thought immediately of the words from the twenty-forth chapter of St Matthew's gospel:

'Then shall two be in the field; the one shall be taken, and the other left.'

Sullock and other fallen friends are commemorated in 'Song of the Dying Gunner AA1.'

> Farewell, Aggie Weston, the Barracks at Guz,
> Hang my tiddley suit on the door
> I'm sewn up neat in a canvas sheet
> And I shan't be home no more.

('Song of the Dying Gunner AA1,' *CP*, p.6 v.4.)

The lines:

> And don't depend on a long weekend
> By the Great Western Railway line

(*ibid.*, v. 3.)

refer directly to Sullock who was born and brought up in a house behind the railway in Newport, a few hundred yards from where Causley was born.

All this death and loss was far in the future. Causley still had to endure the training of a sailor to become a coder, an arcane and unknown craft that was to remain a mystery for some time. Life was hard for a self-confessed 'coward, Puritan and prig' who, nevertheless, was increasingly absorbed by the observation of his fellows. He had to endure such experiences as being ordered to umpire a cricket match on a playing field in the shadow of Brunel's Tamar Bridge. He knew even less of the rules of the game than the 'young Sub-Lieutenant who looked, understandably, on the point of suicide' and who was in charge of the cricket match.

At last Causley's time at Devonport was over. He had been reading *Alice's Adventures in Wonderland* and seeing a lot in common between the surrealist adventures of Lewis Carroll's heroine and his own passage through the Navy. He had another brief weekend leave at home where Causley regaled his family and friends with the utter weirdness of naval life.

His life was to become even stranger as he was posted to Thurso in the extreme north east of Scotland:

"What sort of ship's the 'Thurso'?" I said, anxiously.

"It ain't a ship, it's a place. Didn't you go to school, then?" A sharp look. "Thought not. Next!" (*Hands to Dance and Skylark*, p.176.)

A friend, Ian MacGowan, a 'fresh-faced, square-built Scot; a school-teacher from Glasgow' explained 'with a face like doom' that Thurso was a town in the extreme north of Scotland, "It's where you cross to Scapa Flow," the sound enclosed by the Orkney islands where the German fleet was scuttled at the end of the First World War and a key naval location.

After a forty-eight hour rail journey from Plymouth to Caithness via Euston and Carlisle, Causley emerged from limbo to a Scandinavian landscape and a large meal of bacon and eggs.

'It's all so completely awful: shall I forget nearly bursting into tears in the train lavatory?' (August '40)

A launch took Causley and MacGowan 'towards a narrow slip-pery-looking destroyer of slightly antique trim' which turned out to be HMS Eclipse. Once aboard Causley immediately noticed how quiet the ship was with rows of sailors sitting studying scraps of paper. Were these people coders at work? Far from it; they were engaged in a game of tombola, the navy's only legal form of gambling.

Soon after Causley came aboard the ship sailed. 'An hour later we sailed into the ghastly unknown.' He soon discovered that he was afflic-ted by a particularly violent form of sea sickness:

'Oh that green tossing sea.' (August '40)

He lay for days semi-conscious on the deck beneath the wireless telephone set that he was supposed to operate while others took his turn. When he was conscious he hated the heaving grey ocean with a passion. He loathed everything about the Orkney waters; 'in heaving seas, batter-ing rainstorms, and great slow mists and fogs that oozed despair.' He even hated the sea cliff stacks that loomed up through the mist. He con-sidered the Old Man of Hoy to be 'a pillar at the entrance to hell.' His chronic sea sickness brought him to a closer understanding of his hero Admiral Horatio Nelson who was similarly afflicted at the beginning of every sea voyage.

He fell into a form of despair; obviously he had made a great mis-take in joining the Navy and was totally unsuited to it. Eventually he ral-lied and determined to make the best of it; if Nelson had survived then so could he. He began to observe his shipmates, some of whom had survived the recent Norwegian campaign. They were cheerful under 'a thin veneer of moan and complaint.'

However Causley had yet to find his sea legs:

'Jimmy arising desperately from his hammock, red bursting face, staring eyes. So we are all ill all night and I sit on the lavatory seat in my oilskins and call quietly Mother, I can't stick the seasickness and the thought of going on is impossible: can't read, think, afraid to go below in the fat stinking focstle [sic] so sleep stiffly on the wet floor on an oily overall & some copper wire. An unending nightmare.' (August '40)

He was seasick, homesick and fed up, still wallowing in the depths of self pity:

'I am unwashed, unshaven, dirty, thin, wild, haggard – a horrid sketch of Mother's little boy.' (August '40)

His only form of relief was reading when he was able; Thurber and Muggeridge sustained him at the time. As the ship neared its first port of call the sea calmed somewhat and Causley was able to take his mind off his woes for the first time in weeks. His diary does not say where that first port was but, by his description, it appeared to have been Gibraltar.

' … brown mountains & white square houses dotted on them. The town itself at first dull, silent, & oppressive. There is a crouched air of tenseness hanging over the whole place, & in the narrow streets the smell of tobacco smoke. In the chapel are regimental colours & a hand-blown organ. I kneel & say a small prayer for Mother and home.' (August '40)

On dry land Causley attempted to re-establish the life he had known at home. He bought a number of books, a dressing gown, and two worn cigarette holders that cost him 6/-. He saw the medical officer about his seasickness and was told that he could be transferred to a larger ship and given pills. In the company of two friends, Jimmy and Ivor, he enjoyed his leisure time ashore.

'J and I buy 1/- worth of doughnuts and sit beneath a tree in the cool at the far end of the town eating. Sweat tremendously – 2 cups of oxo.' (September '40)

His sweet time ashore was soon to end.

'Away on Friday … and I experience that terrible sinking of the heart. The sea is glassy & there is a distant whale & the bosun pipes.' (September '40)

HMS Eclipse was steaming south into the tropics and the coast of Africa.

'We are proceeding to Y. but steaming in the opposite direction as a precaution' [against U boats]. (September '40)

Causley was coming to terms with motion sickness at last and his diary entries revert to blue ink. He was reading Vera Brittain's *Testament of Youth* and so missed seeing sharks and flying fish. His summary shows a marked contrast to his former state of intense self pity.

'I am a bit weak at the knees, but survive successfully all but one choppy day when I am ill & sick over the side 4 times after every meal.' (September '40)

He was finally responding to the doctor's treatment.

'Belated pills, cascara (which gives me a bad evening of diarrohea [sic] & I have to go 3 times a day for medicine – probably quinine.' (September '40)

The coast of the dark continent finally appeared on the horizon. HMS Eclipse was arriving in the port of Freetown in Sierra Leone.

'Finally on Saturday is a white lighthouse, palm trees & a gas works which turns out to be camouflaged oil tanks. The mountains are blue & the hills a vivid green, dark, violent, heavy, like a Victorian picture post-card.' (September '40)

He went ashore 'in a white suit with blue edges lent by Shuttle-worth.' His sense of the ridiculous had begun to return as he visited:

' ... the raffish cathedral. George Washington guides me for 1*d*, I give him 2*d*. Black erratic choir practice in the cathedral.' (September '40)

The sultry tropical heat was becoming a problem.

'Scrawl home Tuesday 17th with sweat actually running off me onto the paper.' (September '40)

On shore Causley constantly sought out the elements of his old life in Cornwall.

'Sea bathing, bus through the most beautiful country. Trains come round the corner in the middle of the road.' (September '40)

'8 of us to the – for morning service – 'O Worship the King' & 'Immortal Invisible' with L & J and I singing like birds.'

'At bookshop buy writing paper, notebook for poems & one for stories.'

'Play the piano in the cinema after supper on the – [censored].' (above 3, October '40)

Causley had an interesting encounter with a man who had met Lawrence of Arabia, T. E. Lawrence, the enigmatic archaeologist, Arabic scholar and desert guerrilla fighter:

'There is a cook who met T. E. Lawrence "a small man who gave the impression of power. You felt you were in the presence of somebody who could do things. He behaved like a middy[10] on a ship, there was reserve about him. They called him 'Tim Shaw' & he sat in a corner of the mess with his own radiogram writing a letter." This was at Mount Batten RAF Station in Plymouth. And he saw him come down the Hoe on his motorbike with Lady Astor on the back.' (October '40)

He heard some bad news on the radio:

' ... the wireless says there have been bombs on Cornwall & Chamberlain has resigned & that Churchill is now leader of the Conservative Party.' (October '40)

There is the first specific reference to a poem written by Causley:

'Write to Mother & Russell & send sonnet of 'The Bridge'[11] to P & Wkly News.' (October '40)

His observations in the West African port were still tinged by homesickness:

'The sight of a fire burning red & the bedraggled family assembled for some sort of tea makes me homesick.' (October '40)

He noticed a 'terribly pale yellow, t.b. girl' in 'the drastic heat.' On a Sunday thirteen letters came from his mother along with a parcel of books. Churchgoing became of increasing importance to Causley, not least because it was a link with home.

'Tabernacle on Sunday ... collection plate. David and I put in 3*d* each & a female steward says "Sixpence!" in an appreciative, piercing tone to her neighbour in the midst of thanksgiving.'

'Communion at 10.30. Free Church service at 8.30.' (both October '40)

All too soon Causley and HMS Eclipse were back at sea heading for another African port.

'The old sensations return: headache with too much reading. Seasick pills (too late) & horrid lurching & swaying, especially in the dark ill-lit mess. One day I am cook, & have to go out & be sick in between peeling onions – tears streaming unoriginally down my face.' (October '40)

He describes the joy of approaching land once again:

'The sun on the water, smoke (many colours), half built boats, coloured funnels, gulls, workmen, really lovely cranes & too bright flags are like a Turner painting & too good to be true.' (October '40)

---

10 A 'middy' is a midshipman, the lowest commissioned rank in the Royal Navy, an officer considered callow and wet behind the ears.

11 'The Bridge to Bramblepark' was to become Causley's first published poem.

Once ashore the usual important leisure activities are recorded: cinema, food, coffee and books all keep Causley happy and free from introspection. He notes the death of Neville Chamberlain with the reproduction of a lively conversation on the subject:

1st Sailor (20): "So 'e's croaked it at laust."

Me (23): "Who?"

1st S: "Chymberlin. (reminiscently) Poor ole bawstid.

Seventy two."

2nd S (40): "Three score years & ten. Well 'e 'ad 'is time."

1st S: "Blokes like me & you'll 'ave to steam to get up to 72 what with f- ups by blokes like 'im." (November '40)

Rumours of a posting to Gibraltar were rife and unsettling if they turned out not to be true.

'Life is full of mercurial feelings (mainly good) about the impending change.' (November '40)

Causley had finally reached the turning point; there was no going back to his former rather dull civilian life and he was beginning to form real friendships in the Navy. He mentions a new friend named Frank, 'a great lad and a Xtian [sic].' Finally he admits: 'I have had to abandon homesickness.' Enough of the old life has finally established itself in the new that Causley admitted:

'I am happy at last. I don't regret it – no, never!' (November '40)

Finally the Gibraltar posting became a reality; Causley and his friends were ashore and, naval duties aside, life was becoming varied and fulfilling once again. In December 1940 Causley was briefly admitted to hospital with a chest infection, a situation he turned to his own advant-age by playing the hospital piano. Soon he was swamped with too many commitments in his spare time:

'Took too much on: choir, hospital, pantomime, concert party, & then putting real attention to none, merely shoving one against the other.' (December '40)

Nevertheless he played the piano, the accordion and a 'scratchy old fiddle successfully.' Contacts with Launceston sometimes popped up in unlikely places.

'Wednesday, Frank & I are in the Gib, & we get up to pay & there comes towards me John Dyer who says: "Excuse me, but are you from C'wall?" I say: "Yes – by Jove, from Launceston, & so do you – Prockter & Kents." [ironmongers in Southgate Street.] This excites me greatly.' (December '40)

1940 crept almost unnoticed into 1941.

'I am on watch, & suddenly, an officer pokes his head round the door & says "Happy New Year, old chap." & it is 1941.' (January '41)

One of Causley's New Year resolutions was to learn Spanish. His interest in the Spanish Civil War and Gibraltar's proximity to Spain made this a logical choice. There was also a change of accommodation; Causley would have liked to have shared a cabin with Frank, with whom he had a lot in common but who had reservations about him. In the end he shared with a friend named George. All was not lost: 'Oh the pleasure of my new bed!' (January '41) Friends were very important to Causley; by his own admission he was aware that he had the capacity to lose friendships by his sometimes caustic tongue and occasionally argumentative nature. He was soon to fall out with Frank in Gibraltar.

'Frank and I can work up no interest or enthusiasm for whatever & – see my earlier notes – in my first few weeks couldn't even go to the lavatory without him.' (January '41)

Causley and his friends were aware, in their all male environment, of the possibility of homosexuality. In general they were not in favour of same sex physical love:

'Wally and I are coming through the dockyard, & the tall man in civilian clothes comes along below us, and his behaviour makes me say afterwards "I believe he's on the game." Wally says with Welsh accent "I nearly clouted him with the sauce bottle."' (January '41)

Exposure to all types and conditions of mankind forced Causley to consider the themes of innocence and experience. It was to form one of the cornerstones of the development of his poetry.

An unpleasant petty officer known as 'Nigger' tried to make Causley's life unpleasant by picking on him; Causley was forced to report him in order to put an end to this harassment. This irritating victimisation must have reminded Causley of certain bullies in his primary and secondary schools in Launceston. Because of his unmilitary demeanour he made an obvious target for bullies and men with inferiority complexes. His fastidious and sensitive nature must have made some of his colleagues think of him as a bit of a mother's boy or even a 'nancy boy.' He had the support of his friends and this made his life bearable and enjoyable at times.

'Roddy and Frank and I have our photos taken in the Alameda Gdns. and the result is rather a snowy landscape although it is a bleak day.' (March '41)

Able Seaman Causley and his friend Frank buy oranges at the Alameda Gardens in Gibraltar.

(Special Collections Library, Exeter University.)

Good things continued to arrive from home: 'Parcel with ginger and saffron cake and chocolate arrives sweet and fresh.' News of his friends constantly arrived. Denis was to get a commission and: 'Ginger goes in the Navy on Monday (10th March) which depresses me horribly.' Music played an increasingly major part in Causley's life, saving him from his usual demons of homesickness and depression.

'I write home & the Spanish workman neglects repairing the galley sink & instead tunes & plays my guitar which, he says, is "no f- good."' (March '41)

He continued to observe the foibles of his friends:

'Cliff Dartwell, the coder on watch with me, was an insurance agent & on watch draws dirty pictures and colours them.'

'Relations with Frank now on the old basis, will it last? He still takes Daily Telegraph points of view: cf: concession telegrams & democracy.' (both March '41)

On Wednesday 19th March 1941 Causley qualified fully as a coder, although he was not to be paid as such for some time. He had been in the Navy for just over nine months and would soon be promoted to 'Killick,' or Able Seaman.

'We appear as request men before the Capt. of the Cormorant. When my name is called I double smartly up, slip on the wet deck & land in a heap in front of the Captain's table. I pick myself up, scarlet, & don't know whether to say "Sorry" or what. Anyway, I salute shakily & stand in great agony of surpressed nervous laughter, biting my lip, while he tries not [sic] to stop laughing and reads a blank paper.'

'[I] write home (my "promotion" letter) & can't think of much to say.' (both March '41)

With his sense of humour mostly restored Causley was still hedging his bets about his future happiness: 'No depression or homesickness these days – this may mean a violent attack soon – it usually does.' (March '41)

After two attempts a good photograph was finally taken of Causley and friend at the Alameda Gardens.

'Frank and I have our pictures taken buying oranges off a barrow, & it comes out clear and sharp like a magazine photograph – surprisingly natural and good.' (March '41)

More news came from home, some good, some tragic. Jean wrote after a long silence.

'She says she has been reading my old letters & "somehow I imagine you are a very different Charles these days." I've been very unkind not to write to her.' (March '41)

Reggie Lashbrook, an old friend who worked in the office with Causley, had accidentally fallen one hundred and twenty feet into a quarry while out shooting and was killed aged nineteen. The article from *The Western Morning News* arrived in a letter from home. Causley was much saddened by the news of his friend's death:

'I think of our trips to Looe, Lifton Down, Lakefield & can't really believe he is dead. Wrote letter to Mr & Mrs Lashbrook and mother.' (March '41)

Causley was beginning to be known on the base as a man who wrote poetry. He had submitted a number of sonnets to the local magazine *The Rock*.

'Return bedraggled & slightly bad tempered & take Frank and Roddy's jokes about the dirt on my face (my raincoat still exudes it) & my bad language – with bad grace. Officer at P.O. Savings Bank then asks me if I am the one who writes sonnets – he has seen them whilst censoring letters, & fawns horribly.' (April '41)

Causley's comfortable bed turned out to be infested by bugs: 'Bugs in bed – full and bloody ones.' Much bloodier to Causley was the news that Plymouth was being bombed on a nightly basis in April 1941. He had relations in the city and Launceston lay less than twenty five miles to the north-west. Thoughts of home came flooding inevitably back at Easter tide:

'So glad I came & think of Trusham & St Thomas; and of Kitchener & the National School in 'The Strife is O'er.' (April '41)

References to Causley's work, coding and decoding on different watches became more numerous as did remarks on how well or badly he got on with his close circle of friends.

'Relations with Roddy are strained since he twisted my arm on Sunday – to make me drop a shaving brush & I got annoyed and blasphemous: 'Christ in his Blazing Heaven!' – an old curse. I'm very weary.'

'I am bad tempered because Cliff (quite rightly) got sent off watch instead of me.'

'On watch at 8 … I always get short tempered & snap at Frank & breathe steel at Cliff when we are busy.' (above 3, April '40)

Usually Causley's relations with his friends were harmonious. Many of them made a point of bringing him tea or cocoa in bed in the mornings because they realised how miserable he usually was when he woke

Able Seaman Causley enjoying some time off in Gibraltar.

(Special Collections Library, Exeter University.)

up. He complained of constant tiredness and was a phenomenal sleeper.

'Denis brings me a fez from Tangier, & everyone tries it on.

... talk to Frank of religion and heaven.

I laugh at my own jokes more than I do theirs. Also R says: 'You are a queer mixture – sometimes your thoughts are so lofty & others – well!" (April '41)

He even tried to get on with his nemesis while at the same time taking the mickey:

'In the lavatory, I try & be nice with Nigger (my enemy) because it is Sunday & the sun is shining, with "Been busy?" (very brightly).' (April '41)

He doesn't record what 'his enemy's' reply was. In similar mischievous vein Causley recorded an encounter with a newspaper boy:

'A small Gibraltarian boy is selling newspapers & I imitate him by bawling out "El Calpense a de boy." Said boy (angrily), Bollicks.' (April '41)

Letters from home continued to be very important.

' ... Vera's wedding letter, with photographs. I don't notice Mother at first in it – until Vera says "There is someone in it you'll enjoy looking at." Mother looks neat & clean & bright as ever. Shoes shining & younger looking. I'm delighted with it, & keep looking at it.' (April '41)

Thoughts of home were always with him.

'We bathe – Bob, Dougie, Denis & I – at Catalan Bay, which smells a bit, but has fishing boats & looks rather like a Cornish fishing village (Crackington?)' [Haven] (April '41)

Work was becoming increasingly important and Causley was sensitive to criticism even when apparently deserved: 'Told off by Parsley for learning Spanish on watch rather than reading coding books.' (April '41)

The two chief petty officers in charge of watches were the laconic Parsley and the more sympathetic Bloomfield.

'The best thing is, that the people who read Edgar Wallace or May Edgington on watch & don't try to do what is considered "intelligent" get not a word said! Bloomfield says, "Call em coders? Tell em to take the badges off their arms & stick em up their arse!"' (April '41)

Causley was mastering his coding skills while religiously writing his diary. His spelling and punctuation were not quite perfect; he had not yet mastered the appropriate use of the apostrophe and his spelling was occasionally erratic: 'Bungy asks me, rather surprisingly "How do you spell Brassiére?"' [sic]. Two events loomed up in Causley's immediate future, one possible, the other definite:

'Gibraltar under threat of German invasion. I secretly worry in case the Navy evacuates Gib & I am one of a skeleton staff left behind, & my heart is heavy. I get mentally childish & think, "Oh! I want to see my mother again."' (April '41)

He learned that one of his sonnets had been published in *The Rock*, The magazine published in Gibraltar for local readership.

'The sonnet about the bridge at Bath's Fields (they've called it "Cornwall") is in the April "Rock" magazine, in the midst of a Spanish lesson … & I smoke a cigarette of pride over it.' (April '41)

The poem, actually entitled 'The Bridge at Bramblepark' had been finished on 1st October 1940, submitted and forgotten; it is little wonder that Causley was unable to remember the exact title. It is written at the beginning of his fifth diary in a neat hand quite soon after publication:

"The Bridge at Bramblepark"
I know a bridge among familiar trees
That lean in youthful consort with a brook
And here, hair ruffled by a friendly breeze,
Long have I sat or lingered with a book
Heard & half-heard the singing of the stream,
The tune that small birds tongue, the drowsy bee,
The branches rustling in a long green dream
And the church clock chime its eternal three,
Watched the slim heron on a paper sky,
The fish flash at a shadow, and anew
All this is one – the stream, the fields & I –
And peace comes dropping the whole valley through

There are wild bells of thought within my brain
That ring me to that bridge, that brook, again.

Causley's first published sonnet has little flashes of individuality but is largely derivative, with a nod to Rupert Brooke. It is a competent poem replete with nostalgia for home. Causley still had to develop his distinctive style but the process had begun. He was rarely to use an abab rhyme again. His own evolving style would be much bolder and more experimental; he was, however, establishing the pattern of writing about the past from the point of view of someone whose circumstances had changed.

Causley was often moved to tears by a play or a piece of music and made no secret of it. He was affected by the film *It's a Date*: 'A tear trickles down on my knee, & I remember seeing it at Skegness and being equally moved.' (April '41) We suspect that the remembrance of Skegness helped to produce an extra tear or two.

Chief Bloomfield had taken Causley under his wing and was determined to make a coder of him. We suspect that even Chief Parsley had a soft spot for the serious and gangling Causley.

'Bloomfield held me in the bathroom with a conversation on what he calls "propergander." Frank says, when I laugh at cockney accent, that mine is just as bad – terribly w. country – & I don't sound my aitches.'

'CYS [Chief Yeoman Signaller] Bloomfield amazes me by coming in the cabin & sitting on the bed & asking for a book – short stories or "properganden" pamphlets. He takes Douglas Reed on Strasser. This is the excitable, nervous, original chief who has always treated me well, although he's considered a bit mad & not popular really. But I like him. CYS Parsley appears in the doorway: "How are you Chief?" says I. Parsley: "As usual. Drunk," & chuckles.'

'Parsley says "How's it coming for Leading Coder, Jan? And I say "Fine!" & change the subject. It isn't, of course – I haven't done a thing.' (above 3, May '41)

Causley was universally known as 'Jan' in the Navy because he came from the Westcountry. Strictly a 'Janner' is someone from Plymouth; to an upcountry ear the twenty five miles between Plymouth and Launceston were of little significance.

Soon Causley was to begin studying the coders' book in earnest and his friends encouraged him to keep it up. Frank, the moodiest of his friends and the one who was the hardest to get along with, said a strange thing one evening:

'Frank says (with no trace of perversion – a clean statement) that if I were a woman & had the same mind & behaviour he'd marry me. "This isn't a proposal" says Frank.' (May '41)

Causley's friends were a great support to him as well as an occasional source of intense irritation. They were: Roddy Short, Ginger Crocker, Bungy Lloyd, George Lee, Dougie Mitchell and John Newton, among others. Denis was an old friend who had just become a naval officer by coming up through the ranks. He had a house on the Rock and was a little shy with his former mates, at first concealing his officer's rings from them by putting his arms behind his back. Causley was impressed by his beautifully tailored suit and was glad that the group of friends would continue to meet at his house for a cup of tea and a chat.

Roddy, now fully forgiven for his bad manners, played a joke on Causley:

'Roddy chalks "Jew" on my cabin door & is greatly amused. I feel fairly distinguished (Chaplin?) & leave it on.' (May '41)

Charlie Chaplin had always been happy to be perceived as Jewish when, in fact, he was not. Both he and Causley tacitly acknowledged the rich Jewish artistic, musical and cultural contribution to western civilisation. Causley also did a pretty good impression of Chaplin:

'I did Charlie Chaplin imitations – danced with broom, and 2 sailors' caps.' (July '41)

The news from home came frequently and sometimes had the power to worry Causley:

'Letter from home – 22nd April [1941] is a happy one. I stop short at the bit where Terence Blank is missing & feared drowned – & groan. And then read – 2 lines later – that on the following Monday came a wire saying that he had been picked up & was all right.' (May '41)

However Causley's Aunt Mabel [nee Bartlett] had died in Launceston.

'I feel my old life breaking & falling in pieces. Aunt Mabel died at 4.45 am 24th April. Quiet, jokey, cursed a bit – used to call me "Charm" like Uncle Bill.' (May '41)

Other news concerned the progress of the war.

'On the way back through the town there are many drunks in the dark, singing, piddling, etc. & I slip on somebody's sick. When I get up, Frank says "Hess is dead – Rudolf Hess." … "One less of the bastards" says George Lee.' (May '41)

They were soon to hear that bastard Hess was not dead but in custody in Scotland.

Causley was upset because many of his friends were going home on leave and he had to stay to take his exam. Ralph was due eighteen days leave and no doubt boasted to Causley of past and future sexual conquests. This made Causley feel rather sour and Ralph replied:

'Then, after an account of an "extremely youthful passion" he says "But I have forgotten, you are more or less one of these woman haters so I won't bore you with the other details."' (May '41)

Causley was certainly no 'woman hater' but he could be rather prim at times and was probably fed up with hearing Ralph's boastful account of how he intended to spend his leave, a sore point at the time with Causley. Because he was not boastfully lustful his mates categorised him as different from themselves.

John Dyer was due to go on leave very soon. He was a link with home, coming as he did from Launceston.

'But it is someone from Lanson, & I do feel that someone here from Lanson alleviates mother's pain at my continued absence, & certainly my own.' (May '41)

More links to home came from a friend named Escott:

'Escott is there (from Exeter) says he went to Teignmouth, with his friend called Tancock – who had relatives there called Causley. "Lived in a house in a street parallel to the sea front" says E. I want to ask him more questions, but decide not to as he is a quiet sort & anyway I talk too much.' (May '41)

Revision continued at an accelerated pace as the 13th June leading coders' exam approached.

'Parsley gives me some old coding exam papers, which scare me. "It ain't all revvylant, though" says Parsley.'

'Cliff says of Parsley "He swears in a nasty way – he don't even laugh with it."' (May '41)

The news that Causley's second poem ('The Swimmers') hadn't yet been published in *The Rock* was vastly overshadowed by the terrible news of the sinking of HMS Hood.

'The "Hood" has been blown up – hit in the magazine by a shell from the Bismarck. "If I'd been on her I'd ha' thought it was the safest ship in the world" people say bitterly, and: "There were over 100 boys on her."' (May '41)

The tragic loss of HMS Hood had a profound effect on Causley which his surviving friends mention today. There were only three survivors from a crew of nearly fifteen hundred.

A verbal snapshot reveals Causley's state of mind at the time.

'Bob's boorishness makes me want to scream & kill him. I am writing this rather more neurotically than life because it is now 2 in the morning & I am tired. I am in the lavatory behind the Police Club & suddenly see the plough in the sky. Remember how I used to see it walking down Wooda Lane, [in Launceston] & sometimes stop & admire: Well, it's here too.' (May '41)

Soon came the news of the sinking of the Bismarck with even

greater loss of life than when the Hood went down. News also came from home:

'Mother writes of a German plane on exhibition on the Castle Green. "It ought never to be given a place like that for exhibition – horrid thing."'

'Ginger says Eric Sullock's minesweeper hit a mine, but it didn't go off.'

'Russell [Uren] is a cook.' (above 3, May '41)

Causley had now been in the Navy for a year and celebrated by drinking too much. A horrible hangover was the result. On the positive side was that Ellerton was able to repair his reading lamp once more; Causley no longer had to read himself to sleep with a candle. He still encountered delicious coincidences that appealed to his by now well tuned sense of the ridiculous.

'Collings (of Peter's office [in Launceston][12]) is a seaman. Harry Medland, on his way to Egypt, stopped at a port where it was very hot & a "nigger came out in a top hat and nothing else" – in a canoe. "I wonder if it's the one you describe at Freetown? This is cute – because I'm pretty sure it is.' (May '41)

Back home Jean was in hospital recovering from appendicitis. She and Causley continued to correspond. Plymouth had been extensively bombed, the city centre lay in ruins, but the evacuees had not yet arrived at Causley's mother's house in Tredydan Road.

'Mother says, bravely, to the man: "I want to keep the sitting room for my son if he comes home."' (June '41)

Occasional bombing attacks on Gibraltar began as Causley revised for his coder's exam causing the men to run, tin hats in hand, to an underground tunnel.

'Swot for an hour after supper & how I hate it.'

'When there is an air raid, their maid Maria (at Rosia) leans out of the Window & cries "Arriba Inglaterra!" Alf, meanwhile, under the table.' (above 2, June '41)

The possibility of death came to the forefront of everyone's minds:

'We are looking at tombstones, later, & Joney says one of his earliest recollections is going into a churchyard in Wales with a small cousin. They had just learnt to read, & slowly deciphered "Not dead, but sleeping" on a tomb – & both fled in a terrible panic.'[13] (June '41)

---

12 Otto Peter was a well known Victorian architect in Launceston.

13 This diary entry reminds us of Causley's childhood adventures in St Thomas' churchyard, later to be described in the poem 'By St Thomas Water.'

Causley had a prophetic dream about his friend Eric Sullock who left Launceston on the same train for training in Skegness and who was to die in the Atlantic:

'An extraordinary clear dream: I am at barracks again, lots of recruits in civvy clothes, & meet Bowden's errand boy, aged 20, (haven't seen or thought of him for years) & Eric Sullock. We go home for 4 days & I am amazed & incredulous at my luck. Walking across the Castle Green – it had become a cemetery, & the Castle ruins are thinner & more fallen down. Tombstones up by Doomsdale Gate.' (June '41)

Finally the dreaded day of the exam arrived, after a couple of postponements, it was Friday 27th June 1941.

'The terrible day dawns. The theory in the morning is searching, but fairly easy, & we walk to Rosia in the sun quite jubilantly. At 1 the practical: a horrible paper, much stuff we normally do not handle, & I shake horribly when he says "Only 15 minutes more," and can't find a thing, & lose my nerve completely.' (June '41)

Causley and his friends went out to try to forget their woes.

' … & on to Camp Bay: rocky like Cornwall, through dusty archways, past sentry & through barbed wire, down a long wooden flight of steps to the stony beach. The rock rises sheer with building on the top like the Foreign Legion.'

'Gib. Really does look like an old crouching lion.' (both June '41)

Two days after the exam Causley received some good news:

'When I go on watch at 12, George Dean shakes me by the hand, & they tell me I've passed the exam: which excites & stuns me.' (June '41)

He was now a 'Killick,' or Leading Coder and had to buy the badges to sew on his sleeves. Being a cautious man, Causley did not write to tell his mother the good news straight away. He waited to be notified initially; when this did not happen he delayed the news for a few more days until he was quite sure of his promotion. He still fell prey to nostalgia from time to time.

'As I write this John McCormick singing "Silent Night" – a tune that always takes me to the tight misery of the "E" [HMS Eclipse] days – always the last record they played before we turned in.' (July '41)

Causley was experiencing problems with his friend Frank who seemed to have leanings towards homosexuality:

'F[rank] is, I think, hyper-sensuous – likes to lie naked on the beach, & imply in a Boy-Scoutish way, let's all be manly & do likewise which drives me from the complete emancipation from nakedness – fear of my destroyer days – where, bathing in a bucket, we were completely disinterestedly naked & unashamed – to a horror stricken Puritanism, trying to be "decent" & "manly" & it makes me sick with disgust.' (July '41)

He tries to understand the attraction of men to men:

'F comes & talks with great honesty & a kind of tortured charm (I am flattered that he tells me) about his jealousy at B's relations with J. I could never talk about myself so honestly & greatly admire it. He is worried because he finds himself "less disgusted at that sort of thing" than when he joined the Navy first. This is difficult to write about properly. His essential decency gives him hell, but much less hell than the other thing. What we all need is a pretty girl to talk to & take out to tea.' (July '41)

Causley had possibly found that girl, although removed by over a thousand miles from Gibraltar.

'But more exciting is the letter from Jimmy's sister, Mary, – a beautiful, tall girl & not the steel rimmed school marm I expected … '

'I wish desperately Jimmy were here, to ask a lot of questions about this girl, but can only keep looking in a state of wonder at the picture. The trouble is: the letter doesn't really require an answer – but I must somehow.' (both July '41)

It is clear from these diary entries the Causley was not homosexual; he was shy and isolated, quiet and artistic, but not physically drawn to men. If anything his attraction to women was too intense. He felt awkward in the presence of attractive women not because he lacked attraction but because he felt that they were unattainable and he didn't want to make a fool of himself. Other male friends were proving a problem but not necessarily for the same reason as Frank.

'Bob annoys me so much I could poleaxe him: superior ignorance.' (July '41)

'Tubby Watts goes today too, & the sound of his departure rings like music in my ears.' (September '41)

'Letter from Reg. Reg is sometimes a well-off, pompous, churchly ass but very sincere. Calls playing the organ a "service for God." He is a bloody awful organist & really ought to pay them, poor dears.' (July '41)

Causley felt that he had to try harder to control his irritation with some of his colleagues. 'I feel all I want to achieve is good humour & tolerance of all things but the plainly stupid.' (July '41) His good humour was not improved by swarms of jellyfish with painful stings congregating off his favourite swimming beaches, Camp Bay and Eastern Beach. He swam when it was clear but suffered the occasional sting. Others were also indisposed:

'Parsley has diaorrhea [sic].[14] "I'm thinking of bringing a f- book up & settling down" he says bitterly, as I come in.' (July '41)

The unfortunate CYS Parsley was sicker than he thought; he ended up in hospital, his duties taken over by the dreaded CYS "Nigger."

'Nigger, now Pop (Parsley) is in hospital about his ears & nose is dayman & chief of the coders: oh curses! But he's not too bad, & on the surface we are on good terms.' (July '41)

Bob Johnson, never to be confused with the obnoxious Bob, a new friend of Causley's had also passed the coder's exam while Bungy did not. Sid Crofts, from Derbyshire, also became a friend while Frank was often ignored, particularly after he became rather close to Johnnie who seemed to have broken off with B.

Letters arrived from Rattler Morgan who was bobbing about on the cold grey waters of Scapa Flow and from Russell Uren, the conscientious objector from Launceston.

'Russell was given a piece of shrapnel by a small boy in the train, even after telling him what his NCC badge stood for. At first, he says, "I stood condemned & felt it keenly."'

'Mother says "Hitler would soon end the war if he had to take evacuees."' (both August '41)

Laura Causley, in her house in a damp valley bottom in Tredydan Road, had developed rheumatism. She wrote: 'It will pass again soon – rain about I dare say.' (August '41)

There was more bad news from home; Eric Wickett, a Corporal in the RAF, a friend of Causley's and a notable athlete, had been killed in an accident overseas.

' … tall brown youth with the broken, white teeth – friendly & straight – as the dashing Mercutio in "Romeo & Juliet" who – I think – looked more like a real Elizabethan than anyone I ever saw.' (July '41)

The radio also brought more bad news: 'On the news is that the [HMS] Fearless had been sunk: the ship on which, I think, is Escott the coder from Exeter.' (July '41)

Frank was becoming obnoxious and determined to irritate Causley.

'Frank today says to me: "When are you going to stop behaving like a child of three?" because I tell him off for tearing an essay by Robert Lynd out of a New Statesman in the mess. I say "Two! Two!"' (August

---

14 Causley spelt the word 'diarrhoea' three different ways in his diaries, all incorrectly.

Causley celebrated his twenty-fourth birthday by losing his cap in the street. A soldier returned it to him but he found that the ribbon with "HMS Cormorant" had been taken, never to be returned. "Something to remember your birthday by" says Frank optimistically.

Comic photographs were taken of Causley and friends as statues, Chinese executioners and Arabs to be sent to friends and families. These are reminiscent of earlier photographs taken at home of Causley in various theatrical productions. One that comes to mind is Causley in a fez and baggy trousers grinning broadly from the front doorway of 23 Tredydan Road. Some of Causley's friends went home on leave or to other postings.

'Joney went today at 4. This Alun E Jones, the dramatic, swearing Welshman, comedian & lively companion – Yeoman of our watch.'

'Bob J[ohnson] will be going: bald, quiet, rather flat footed & faintly ridiculous. I hate to think of him among old bastards at sea: his place is at home, in the garden with a spaniel & Betty.' (both September '41)

Causley received 4/6d in royalties from Curwens in September 1941. His life was now firmly set into two parts: going on watch as a coder and going to plays, concerts and the occasional party on the Rock. As he became more proficient at his naval job he was able to play greater parts in the concerts and plays which were being produced.

' … then to the "Sacred Heart" where is a concert by the N. Ship's company: ventriloquist who spoils his act by too much swearing. At first it was funny, but – keeping it up – a bore.' (September '41)

The other half of his life also contained considerable feats of swearing, often to good effect:

'Pa Parsley is very excited – obviously going home … P writes notes bequeathing furniture, & instructions about readdressing letters from his wife & destroying them from a couple of mistresses. "If they get 'ome, I'm in the f- divorce court" says he merrily.' (September '41)

Parsley's departing gift to Causley made him very happy.

' … and they give me the writing desk they have made & the green glass reading lamp – which give my cabin a gloomily tremendous distinguished appearance.' (September '41)

Autumn was drawing on and the rainy season approached. Causley read a book he considered remarkable, Harry Price's book on the haunting of Borley Rectory. He talked about the book on watch and shared it with his friends.

'October (when it doesn't rain) is I think the best month in Gib: clear, crisp & a view for miles over the hills in Spain.' (October '41)

October had always been Causley's favourite month at home in Cornwall; home thoughts from abroad. Friends, and the rather gay Frank in particular, still could be a problem to a sensitive man somewhat prig-gish and set in his ways.

'Relations with Frank strained. I ignore & snub him which I know gives him much more hell than ever it does me. The trouble is I think I want to be left quite alone, communicate what experiences I like & not have to answer questions like "Where are you going now [?]" Frank does all this nervously & sharply – a sort of caricature of what I might be like myself if I didn't cultivate an irritating slowness & unconcern.' (October '41)

He realised that what he most disliked in others were the traits that he disliked in his own character.

A new Spanish concert party had come to Gibraltar. Causley and his friends enjoyed and admired Paca Romero, a lively dancer of about forty-five who had very good legs and a wonderful panache. Causley had not lost his appreciation of attractive women.

'I like the twiddly bit in "Rancho Grande" – this is quite unwrite-aboutable.' (October '41)

Under the leadership of Denis a party was organised for the troupe with plenty of drink and music. It proved such a success that Causley considered it one of the high points of his time stationed on the Rock.

Work always came as an unwelcome shock with its irregular hours, lack of sleep, frantic activity between long bouts of boredom. Sometimes the monotony was relieved by an unusual event such as the visit of the Duke of Gloucester.

'We are inspected by the Duke of Gloucester – red faced, in shorts – who walks past rather hastily.' (October '41)

The prospect of advancement and change did not always fill Caus-ley with delight:

'Depressed this afternoon because (after a conversation with Nig-ger) it looks as though I might get my hook & replace him as a dayman in charge of the coding office – which will without doubt send my letter writing & dhobying[15] more to hell than it is at present. I want the hook but not a dayman's job.' (October '41)

He was growing into his rank of Killick, or Leading Coder.

---

15 British slang for washing clothes, from the Hindi word *dhobi*.

'I give the first sarcastic telling off of my career as a Killick, & to my joy even silence Fred.' (November '41)

He occasionally had to report bad news:

'"Ark Royal" down today, & feel depressed.' (November '41)

In December 1941 he became a dayman but still managed his voluminous and constant correspondence. He wrote to Mary Cooke, Ginger, Russell, and, above all, to his mother. His friends were still troubling him; Frank had finally fallen in love with 'J'[ohnny], a young sailor, despite his strong Christian conscience. Causley's disapproval is tangible.

Arthur became his new bête noir, a source of constant and intense irritation:

'Arthur (I'm a vigilante) arrives very drunk, hiccups & staggers & reduces me to a genuine screaming state of nerves – talks for nearly an hour with a fast moon spinning along overhead.' (December '41)

Among his new friends were Simmy and Joe, who would prove rather clinging in a similar way to Frank. One of his most constant friends was Roddy:

'Roddy: tall, clean, sentient, unbusinesslike, the best-hearted – surely – lad of my life & even later than I am for everything. Easily the most individual, extraordinary & nicest lad I've met in the Navy.' (December '41)

News was arriving from the outside world:

'Simmy … he says "Oh, & the Japanese are bombing Hawaii & the Philippine Islands.' [Sunday December 7th 1941] (December '41)

The news from home was more amusing. An airmail letter arrived from Laura Causley with a welcome 10/- note and:

'The wardrobe door fell off this morning "and" the house seemed so small with her (Jean the evacuee) at my elbow all the time.' (December '41)

It seemed that Laura also greatly valued her own space. She dealt with its infringement in the same humorously irritable way as her son.

As 1941 drew to a close on the rainy Rock at Europe's extremity dramatic possibilities were opening up for Causley as his play *Benedict* was read to see if would be suitable for performance. Causley observed that his friend Joe was becoming a little critical in a similar vein to Frank.

'Joe says my most irritating characteristic is saying constantly I can't do something when all the time obviously know I can.' (January '42)

1942 arrived with thoughts of past Launceston Christmas pageants:

' … cold, dark, & little Arthur (an angel with a lighted candle) falls down some steps.' (January '42)

The comparison between past innocence and present experience is obvious. The obnoxious naval Arthur was never far away.

'Arthur (drunk). I avoid Arthur all the time, who tries to bear down on me with terrifically boring conversation about Smithy, &c. (all of which could be said in 6 words), winks, nods & leers, at every opportunity.' (January '42)

In January of 1942 Causley produced his one act play *Benedict*.

'I smoke far too many cigarettes but enjoy the producing immensely.' (January '42)

He also replaced the frequently drunken Selborne on the play committee. A letter from home informed him that his old friend Eric Sullock, who had left Launceston on the same train as Causley, was now on the Russian convoys.

At last Gibraltar was attacked by the enemy:

'Suddenly there is a most appalling explosion, the whole quarters rattle and shake, windows fly open. Then outside (I notice the blackout blown away & hanging): a cloud of brown smoke, the "E" sunk, the "I" burning, the "H" a big gaping hole torn in her side.' (January '42)

Causley's cabin was a mess of plaster dust and disorder. Naturally the reading light had ceased to function. A performance of a variety act failed to cheer Causley up.

' … dislike the crazy violin act by the horrid little man in a purple suit who reminds us of Goebbels & his partner of Frau Goering – broken down, touring the halls after the war.' (January '42)

The performance of Causley's play *Benedict* was a great success, especially since the playwright had to replace Herries, who had to go to sea, in the title role. A brigadier and a major general both enjoyed the play and told Causley so afterwards. A cutting sent to Causley from one of the Launceston papers is dated 13th February 1942:

Local Author at Gibraltar – 'The *Gibraltar Chronicle* of January 29th, contains an account of the production, by the Gibraltar Dramatic Society, of *Benedict*, a one-act drama written by Coder Charles Causley RN, of Launceston. Particular interest was attached to the performance because for the first time the author himself played the leading part. Our congratulations to the author!' (February '42)

It is clear that at this point Causley was doing far too much and spreading himself too thinly. Exhaustion and depression were sure to follow as well as the usual bout of self-criticism.

'I'm doing too much & feel worn out, dirty, tired, a bit drunk, fed up.' (January '42)

News from home was uplifting. Laura had a visit from one of Causley's friends on leave:

'A rat-tat at the door. I went & there stood a sailor in the pouring rain. "I've come from Gibraltar." It is Wolfe.' (January '42)

Laura also continued to complain about her evacuee:

'I notice she's like you used to be – whatever I'm doing she must do as well. When I stopped knitting, she did the same.' (February '42)

Meanwhile Causley had cleaned up his cabin and was glad not to have to share it with any of his friends, some of whom still had the capacity to shock him.

'Wiggy & the nice sparker [electrician] who has shorts & trouble with his accent. Drunk Wimpy, who winks & beams in great old Cockney fashion. They came off shore a bit tight & there are shocking homo-displays which only amuse me now I don't have to live among it – how very easy to laugh it off then. My own room when I get back is a neat solid quiet paradise.' (February '42)

Amusement was caused by Clive who quoted passages from letters he had censored:

' … the priceless collection Clive has made (as a censor) from letters: "I think our love affair has developed into a kind of sacrilege which I shall never desecrate." Etc.' (February '42)

A new run of performances of *Benedict* had been ordered to go along with the boring Security Plays. Causley now had to play the part of Olga and was duly measured for a dress. His friends could not imagine him as a woman and neither could he. Simmy had been sent off to sea worried about his rheumatism. Mrs R was proving a problem with her constant temper tantrums and bouts of inattention.

'Rehearsal: Mrs R playing with Glazier's enormous & awful cat, most of the time, & paying not much attention to the play.' (February '42)

In February 1942 the play was ready, or as ready as it ever would be.

'Ian nearly gets the bird with "Benedict," house restive & shuffly – it is an agony to sit in front & play the piano – & I abandon it after doing my stuff in the right places: creep out & start being made up as Olga.'

'Roberts & I, I think, give really good performances – & put in lines that aren't there ("You British Officers are so stupid" gets a good laugh & round of applause) & I even have a banquet afterwards. But I get terribly drunk & can't be Civilian B, so somebody else reads it.'

'Next performance: when I make my entrance as Olga my cloak catches on a nail in the door – but we recover.' (above 3, February '42)

At this time Causley, realising that he could not accumulate too much paper in his cabin, began burning some of his old letters. A newspaper extract from home gave him pause for thought. In it fellow Cornishman A. L. Rowse had written:

'For a Celt, then, living in an English environment is, I find, a constant struggle with one's temperament.' (February '42)

Rowse was very much a role model for Causley. A brilliant scholar and writer, Rowse came from a humble Cornish background. He was born near St Austell in the Higher Quarter, the highly industrialised Clay Country. Late in the war Causley was to write to Rowse asking for advice on how to become a writer.

There were rare moments of contentment:

'What charm it is to sit in a small room at a small oak table and eat.' (March '42)

All was not always well in Causley's theatrical world, people were increasingly late for rehearsals or did not turn up at all. Some of the actors were downright incompetent.

'[A J] Glazier, when I get back to the Theatre, completely ruins the 2nd Act, & I curse and call him a bloody bastard, which I at first think annoys Miss James – but afterwards discover it probably delights her as she at once begins to call me "Charles".' (March '42)

Later:

'Miss James writes on my programme: "Thank you for all your help – though you had to be so brutally candid at times."' (March '42)

Glazier offered to commit suicide if he messed up the second act again. Causley suggested that he did so during the very last performance of the play.

More bad news came in March 1942.

'At 7. Geoff arrives with tea & the bad news that the "Jupiter" has been lost off Java: "in these narrow seas some survivors possibly got ashore." I cry "No! No!" remembering Dougie Mitchell & Stan, & hoping desperately they are safe & that it really can't be. I can see a burning ship slipping down in a hot sea, with sharks: the pale calm gentle Dougie with the good manners & slow smile, & Stan: probably very frightened, like me.' (March '42)

There was also better news about a more familiar ship:

'Read about the "Eclipse" in the Gib Chronicle: "the navy's most air-raided ship," taking a convoy to Russia, attacking & hitting a German destroyer & returning damaged with the "Trinidad" to port.' (April '42)

Causley now took part in regular broadcasts on the Gibraltar radio. Things did not always go smoothly.

'Took part in broadcast, played piano – but Tipper announces me all wrong & I am infuriated.' (March '42)

In April 1942 Causley was to have played the part of Frederick Douglass in *Lincoln*, a play about the black abolitionist who was instrumental in the run up to the American Civil War.

'Everyone laughs at reading of the horribly difficult part of Douglass, which at first amuses me, then bores me, then makes me angry.' (March '42)

Perhaps it was a good thing that the play was cancelled because Clive, the producer, went home on leave.

Causley was becoming increasingly irascible and complained of pain in his legs and fatigue. He found himself searching for female sympathy.

'I say about the women in the play, that I usually arouse their maternal instincts – "The old maternal." Tommy: "You rather invite it." Me: "Yes, & it's much more difficult than you may think."' (March '42)

His symptoms were developing:

'Head very hot, can't sleep properly, bit of diahhroea [sic].' (April '42)

He eventually went to see the doctor who signed him off and sent him up to the hospital for treatment. He was given pills for abdominal colic, which he considered to be "really Gib stomach" and sent back to his cabin for rest.

'When I get back is the best thing of the day: someone playing Grieg's piano concerto: ringing through the dark empty quarters & in my room: makes bombs even more ridiculous than ever.' (April '42)

Causley's friend Joe, a lance sergeant in the army, had replaced Frank but continued to behave neurotically in a rather possessive way that Causley found irritating and threatening.

'Joe owns up to having written a poem ("It wasn't like yours – it rhymed. But I lost it.") about a conversation on the telephone.' (April '42)

'Joe gives me this telephone poem, which is terribly schoolboyish &

quite awful, & makes my own stuff seem better than it really is.' (May '42)

As he recovered from his indisposition Causley returned to the cares of his Gibraltar posting. A new Chief Yeoman was coming 'who may get my job.'

'Expecting bombs from the French because we have invaded Madagascar.'

'We are in tropical rig today: first thing, everyone in white, the place looks like an American hospital film or a sanatorium.' (both May '42)

Causley's friendship with Joe was waning. He and Joe had little in common; Stanley Simmonds[16] now began to fill the space left by Frank and Joe. Stan was a far less neurotic person and totally "straight," and a very talented artist. He had a fiancée named Morwenna to whom Causley wrote a poem when Stan was in hospital finally having his tonsils out.

'Only good line: that prodigal memory spills from uncertain pockets.' (May '42)

Later:

'Stan arrives at 11 with letter from Morwenna ("I found the last 2 lines a wee bit obscure – but it is a lovely thing taken all round") which at first sends me into a small panic as I wrongly imagine her taking it round to all her friends. Also I laugh at "he must have thousands of friends."' (May '42)

Encouraged by contact with a woman Causley rather went "over the top":

'We go ashore at 7 & drink in the Winter G[ardens] & Theatre Bar & Grand very bad sherry & whisky lime & lemon. Pick up Grace & Betty & Co, & to the dance. I dance about 2, then pass out, kiss Grace a lot & am then promptly very sick. Can't remember much.' (May '42)

The copious ingestion of alcohol temporarily overcame Causley's shyness and awkwardness, but at a price!

'Shocking hangover: cabin in a dreadful state.' (May '42)

Letters from home remained a vital part of Causley's life. In May 1942 his mother was concerned because she had received no letters from him for ten or eleven days. Then, like the London buses, they all arrived together. She wrote back immediately sending an article from the local paper from Saturday March 14th marking twenty five years since the death of his grandmother "Mrs Bartlett of St Thomas, Launceston aged 64."

---

16 Stanley Simmonds was born the same year as Causley and became one of his lifelong friends as well as a well known artist.

She also sent news of Aunt Norah from Trusham:

'Writes mother [sic] – of Norah saying about me. "You aren't supposed to be strong & won't be able to earn your living when you come home."' (June '42)

Closer to home: 'Fred comes up with a camera & says: "Well – Tobruk's gone. We've surrendered."' (June '42)

At this point of the war Great Britain was at its lowest ebb and probably as far from eventual victory as it was ever to be. Even in his "cushy" posting Causley was at considerable risk from unpredictable air raids.

' … sit in the bathroom on a cushion underneath the wash slab & smoke a cigarette. Shrapnel tinkling down like rain in the yard.' (June '42)

Stan came out of hospital and he and Causley had many enlightening conversations.

'We have an absorbing conversation, starting off from Spender writing on D. H. Lawrence, about respecting other peoples' still centre of personality & being aware of the "otherness" in one's fellow men.' (June '42)

Lawrence, in his novel *Kangaroo*, had definitely seen the Cornish as 'other.'

Here we have Causley's problem with close friends. Frank and Joe were both too needy and off balance to become close friends with Causley. Both Frank and Joe seem to have been attracted to Causley in a homosexual way that was definitely not reciprocated. Stan was a balanced character with no homosexual needs and Causley felt relaxed in his company; his "still centre of personality" was not threatened and the two men had much in common on an intellectual level. Stan drew a beautiful drawing of Causley in naval rating's uniform resting on his bed in his cabin in Gibraltar.[17] Causley and Stan were to remain lifelong friends after the end of the war.

Causley's diary entries dispel any hint of homosexuality in his nature. On his own admission he could be sarcastic, temperamental, occasionally somewhat neurotic but never interested in sexual liaisons with men.

'I say: For a month I've seen a hell of a lot of Stan – from 8 in the morning until 11 at night. He doesn't wear on me.

R: Yes – you do tend to 'take people up' don't you.

Me: I've known him since last August – I don't know if that's taking

---

17 To be seen at the Lawrence House Museum in Launceston.

people up.

And: You have to like a person a lot to work with him all day and stick him in the evenings as well.' (July '42)

The "cushy" posting on the Rock could not last.

'S[tan] talks so brilliantly & realistically about his 8 months of completely fantastic life in Devonport Barracks, & reminds me so clearly of my own dreadful misery there, … that I am filled with a macabre dread of the inevitable return there.' (July '42)

As usual Causley was short of money waiting for the next pay parade.

'We are very poor & live in perfect communism: S.[tan] brings – at dinner time – 2*d*. Because he knows I have no money to buy tea with. I take round to him the one packet of cigarettes, etc.' (June '42)

The tedium of endless watches was broken by the official visit of General Barron y Ortiz, Military Governor of Algecieras.

'This we have a grandstand view of. The [British] Consul, in a battered top hat & concertina trousers; the General wearing an enormous green order; the soldiers who have their boots polished by a private – disgusting sight.' (June '42)

A letter from home brought Causley some sadness and reminded him that, in many ways, life was passing him by.

'Joan Bickley is being married next Thursday to a vicar or parson's son – I mean: Methodist. This upsets me a bit & I go & talk to Stan.

I say "I don't know that I ever really intended to marry her, but she was a good queen or jack."

Stan: "But you wouldn't be satisfied with a queen or jack would you?"'

'Mother writes of walking to Newchurches with Dorrie Pethick – which sounds good for a leave. I suddenly think how this girl (and she's married to Albert W.) likes a lot of things I do too, & how for many years I got her wrong because of the P's & the dreadful mother she has.' (both July '42)

From these diary entries Causley emerges as an essentially lonely man. He recorded a humorous conversation with Arthur Heathcote:

'Me: I shall be a quarter of a century next month. Blimey!

Standen: That's nothing – I'm 32.

Me: My father died when he was 37 – I used to think he was quite old.

Arthur: So did mine.

Me: He died after the last war … result of war wounds.

Arthur: So did father.

Me: He was in the … let's see, I forget.

Arthur: Father was in the R.A.S.C.

Me: That's right … R.A.S.C.

Dreadful pause

Me: Arthur – don't tell me he was a Driver?

Arthur: (sigh of relief): No.' (July '42)

The realisation that he would soon be posted elsewhere also meant a period of leave for Causley who had not been home for well over a year.

'Bungy Williams now going – this brings my own departure even closer, although I cheer myself up & laugh talking about suitcases.' (July '42)

A last word on the different relationships with Joe and Stan:

'Meet Joe at 6: we eat in the café at Engineers Lane. Can't think of much to say & it is really a bit strained & deadly, although I looked forward to it. Stan's company is so much deeper & full of variety & truth & flashes of imagination.' (July '42)

The closing days of Causley's posting were full of good companionship and conversations.

'Robert very pleasing & witty & entertaining these days & I regret bitterly he won't be a permanent background to my life.' (July '42)

A newspaper article arrived about Causley's old ship HMS Eclipse:

Honour for 19 in ace destroyer:

'Lieut-Commander Edward March DSC, commander of the Eclipse, one of Britain's "ace" destroyers has been awarded the DSO "for great courage, skill and determination in action while escorting a convoy."

Two of Eclipse's officers get the DSC, six of the crew get the DSM and ten others are mentioned in dispatches.'

With a certain amount of trepidation Causley was now preparing to move. He turned out an old kitbag and found an old pair of forgotten boots at the bottom.

The final few pages of the diary are blank. On the inside of the back cover are written two verses of a poem by A. E. Housman in Causley's neat hand:

The Recruit.

Come you home a hero
Or come not home at all
The lads you leave will mind you
Till Ludlow tower is down

Leave your home behind you
Your friends by field & town
Oh, town & fields will mind you
Till Ludlow tower is down.

Housman's lyrical rural poetry with its sense of loss was to have a great influence on Causley's poetry. Archaic in poetic form, it showed Causley that the old forms were valid and worth pursuing. Because so many of the poets who influenced Causley were either covertly homosexual, like Housman and Sassoon, or openly so, like Auden, many people assume that Causley was of a similar persuasion. Such generalisation is unjust but has done Causley's reputation no harm.

After this point Causley never resumed his diary except for appointments. He returned home to the towers of Launceston on leave, not exactly the conquering hero but as an useful and promoted coder who had experienced a lot but retained his innocence. His life in Gibraltar had mirrored his home life with tedious periods of work relieved by good company, music, a certain amount of mild alcoholic excess and, above all, observation and much reading and drama.

He came home to a town almost devoid of his old friends. Wartime austerity was nothing new and Causley slipped back into his long walks and piano playing at Tredydan Road. He found his mother slightly older and grudgingly putting up with refugees from Plymouth. Like her son she had always very much valued her own space. But there was a war on; Leading Steward Eric Sullock was reported killed on the Russian convoy when his ship, HMS Bredon, was sunk on 8th February 1943.

Causley was never to rejoin HMS Eclipse. The E and F Class destroyer that had been recalled to service at the beginning of the war and had distinguished herself, was sunk by a mine in the Aegean Sea on 24th October 1943. Over three hundred men died, half of them crew, half soldiers.

No doubt missing some of his friends in Gibraltar, Causley longed for the war to end. He knew he would write poems, short stories and plays. He had had some modest success as a published playwright and poet and he was determined to take it further. Many of the themes that would play a great part in his future work were becoming established in his consciousness. The Navy was a great starting point in his writing career.

Causley was posted back to Gibraltar and promoted to Leading Signaller. He may not have resumed his diary for a number of reasons. It is possible that he was reprimanded at some point for keeping it, it could have been confiscated or Causley decided that he had nothing more to record that had not already happened. In any case he obviously took his job seriously because he was promoted to Acting Petty Officer in 1943 roughly two years after becoming a 'killick.' This promotion entitled him to more money and the opportunity to run his own watches. A year later he was 'confirmed' as a Petty Officer. He was to rise no further as the rank of Chief Petty Officer did not exist for Coders.

In 1944 he was at last able to stop wearing what he considered an antiquated and impractical uniform.

' ... I abandoned my round hat and bell-bottoms forever and appeared (in my own estimation) glorious in peaked cap, double breasted suit and brass buttons ... It was a solemn moment when I realised that for the first (and probably the last) time in my life I had reached the top of my profession.' (*Hands to Dance and Skylark*, p.186.)

Causley's rebellious streak caused him to keep his round sailor's hat which he should have handed in. With its ribbon marked 'HMS Cormorant' it sat in his house in later years beside the *Pickelhaube* brought back from France by his father early in the Great War.

As quite a senior coder Causley did not stay in Gibraltar all the time. He sailed on various assignments to various Mediterranean ports such as Malta and Alexandria, bustling exotic places that excited his imagination. It is a pity that his service record is still classified because we do not know very much about the two years between the end of his diary and his posting to HMS Glory, a brand new aircraft carrier, in February 1945 as a 'confirmed' Petty Officer Coder. His voyages around the Mediterranean excited his imagination and prepared him for the exotic and sultry ports of the Far East.

It seemed that the Navy had heeded the early advice of his doctor suggesting a shore or big ship assignment on account of his acute sea sickness and for this Causley was eternally grateful. He was now a member of the Chiefs' and Petty Officers' Mess, 'what some would call the holiest of all holies in the Royal Navy.' He was in awe of some of the chiefs and Petty Officers:

'Sitting in the C. & P.O.'s Mess, listening to the incredible tales of my companions, the more unlikely-sounding stories often the ones more solidly based on fact, I felt even more closely in touch with the days of Nelson and the worlds of Tobias Smollett's *The Adventures of Roderick Random*, *The Adventures of Peregrine Pickle* and the Elizabethan seamen than I had ever been in the old watchkeepers' messes. I viewed the Chiefs and P.O.'s with a wildly romantic eye. To me, in my twenties, they represented the springs of wisdom; they were my Eton, Harrow, Oxford and Cambridge. Between them, they seemed to have been everywhere, and to have tried everything at least once. They spoke of their disasters as well as their successes with a disarming frankness, a kind of half-knowing innocence, and a total lack of concern as to what I, the listener, might think of their (sometimes) appalling revelations. As a secretive Celt, deeply suspicious of the motives of all others, I was amazed, shocked, enthralled. Whether or not I profited by such a prolonged exposure to natural wisdom is another matter.' (*ibid.*, p.187.)

When writing this piece Causley must have had in mind A. L. Rowse, the eminent Cornish historian and writer of the Tudor and Stuart periods. He contrasts his early practical poetic education to Rowse's academic and theoretic preparation.

From his observations and with his keen listener's ear Causley memorised much material for his short stories and early poems. He had moved up the naval 'rooster'[18] and experienced a great deal that was to stay with him for the rest of his life. Had he not had to come to terms with wartime service Causley would have been a very different poet. For the rest of his life he would remain haunted by his profound fear of the might of the sea and of exposure to the cold. The sense of loss at the death of friends and wartime colleagues never left him; the contrast between innocence and experience sometimes made him doubt that mankind would use its free will in the search for its own redemption. Although an agnostic in his teens Causley believed in God more than in mankind. Sorrowful rather than cynical he would never quite reconcile what men did to one another in war and in peace.

---

18 Roster.

Bugis Street

While Causley was decoding in Gibraltar and sailing around the Mediterranean a huge ship was being built in Northern Ireland that would play a major part in his naval career and his transition from sailor to writer and poet.

In November 1942 the keel was laid for a ship known as R62 at Harland and Wolff's shipyard in Belfast. It was to be a Colossus class Light Fleet Carrier and while Acting Petty Officer Causley was doing his watches in Gibraltar or sailing around the Mediterranean hundreds of welders, boilermakers and shipwrights were building the huge ship whose future would be very much bound up with Causley's.

On 27th September 1943 R62 became HMS Glory after her launch into Belfast Lough by Lady Cynthia Brookes, wife of the prime Minister of Northern Ireland. In February 1945 there arrived: 'The draft in February of a thousand matelots[19] from Devonport' which included Petty Officer Causley, no doubt glad to be away at last from the:

… convict air of the Royal Naval Barracks at Devonport

('Chief Petty Officer,' *CP*, p.14 v.1.)

After fitting out and sea trials were completed the brand new aircraft carrier was commissioned on 2nd April 1945 and destined to sail to the Far East to bring the Japanese to their knees.

Turning my face from home to the Southern Cross,
A map of crackling stars, and the albatross.

('HMS Glory,' *CP*, p.7 v.5.)

---

19 'Matelot' is a French word for a sailor used as a slang term in Britain.

The carrier was 695 feet (212 metres) long with a beam of 80 feet (24 metres) and a displacement of 13,400 tons. Powered by four steam turbines her top speed was 25 knots (46 kilometres an hour). Her complement was 13,000 including the air group who maintained and flew the 48 aircraft on board. 837 Naval Air Squadron flew Barracudas and 1831 Naval Air Squadron flew Corsairs; both types of aircraft were equipped with folding wings to facilitate movement up to the flight deck from the vast hanger below.

After being fitted out HMS Glory left Greenock on the Clyde, sailed through the Mediterranean to Alexandria, through the Suez Canal, put in briefly at the ports of Colombo and Trincomali on the east coast of Ceylon in July 1945, finally arriving in Sydney under the 'map of crackling stars' in August. In his long poem 'HMS Glory at Sydney' Causley captured the new sights and, above all, the excitement of going ashore in a strange new city:

And there is no thrill
With a clean shirt and with pound notes in your pocket.

Like stepping ashore in a new country

('HMS Glory at Sydney,' *CP*, p.8 v.6.)

Here we see a confident Causley, experienced in the ways of the Navy and able to enjoy a run ashore. He noticed a particularly attractive barmaid named Janie and the films and plays that were on at the time. All the elements of his former life were there:

The books I bought at Angus & Robertson's bookshop,
Sir Osbert Sitwell,[20] and Q[21] [Sir Arthur Quiller-Couch] (to remind me of home).

(*ibid.*, v.14.)

Unusually for Causley he wrote 'HMS Glory at Sydney' in blank verse. This poem remarkably resembles extracts from his earlier diaries; he even obliquely refers to them:

20 Sir Osbert Sitwell was a well-known Derbyshire writer, poet and art critic.
21 Sir Arthur Quiller-Couch was an eccentric Cornish writer, poet and literary critic at the University of Cambridge.

O Sydney, how can I celebrate you
With a bookful of notes and old letters?
Sitting here in Cornwall like an old maid

(ibid., v.7.)

We will return to Causley's nostalgia for a past that was imposed on him. For the moment we can clearly see that a few days ashore in Sydney were a great relief from:

Our bows scissoring the green cloth of the sea,

(ibid., v.2.)

In August 1945 HMS Glory weighed anchor for the Pacific Ocean and the horde of Nippon. On August 6th an American bomber named for the pilot's mother dropped an atom bomb on Hiroshima. A few days later another cutely named atom bomb devastated Nagasaki. This was, undisputedly, the end of the Great East Asian Co-Prosperity League. Perhaps the bombs halted the Japanese resistance to invasion; an estimated million and a half American lives were saved by the end of the Japanese insistence of fighting to the last man standing.

In various islands the Japanese commanders dressed in their best uniforms and handed over their swords to the victors. Some then committed suicide, others joined the modern world. For the first time the defeated Japanese people saw that their emperor Hirohito was no longer a god but merely a tired and vanquished warlord.

Exactly one month after Hiroshima HMS Glory lay off Rabaul 'off the steaming island of New Guinea' to take the surrender of the Japanese forces in the south west Pacific area; 180,000 soldiers would lay down their arms to the Australian Commander-in Chief of Land Forces, Lieutenant General Sturdee. Causley was there 'in a gleaming, white tropical suit' with the rest of the ship's company to witness the surrender.

'I had a nasty moment when the squad of high-ranking Japanese naval and army officers, the latter in jungle green and trailing swords, were brought up in the aircraft lift to the strident ringing of its bell, and the ship was there to take the surrender of the Japanese forces in that closely guarded by Royal Marines armed with sub-machine-guns. As they were marched at a brisk pace between our ranks, my knees, somewhat

Recently promoted Petty Officer Coder Causley on H.M.S. Glory, April 1945.

(Special Collections Library, Exeter University.)

unceremoniously, banged together.' (*Hands to Dance and Skylark*, p.189.)

The only sight of the enemy that Causley had previously had was of about a dozen German submariners captured by the corvette HMS Marigold and landed in Gibraltar to rumours that they were the survivors of the U boat crew that had sunk HMS Ark Royal in the western Mediterranean.

Despite the boat which was to bring the surrender party to the carrier sticking to the side of the mother ship because it had been too thickly painted, the surrender was taken without incident. No kamikaze planes appeared overhead to compromise the ceremony.

' … the Japanese advancing along the flight-deck – no longer paper faces on war-posters or absurd figures in newspaper cartoons, but a very present reality … ' (*ibid.*, p.190.)

The reality of the surrender was overpowering as the terms were read aloud first in English then in Japanese. The whole thing took about an hour. Causley's sense of the ridiculous saved the day for him from being taken too seriously.

'My friend Chief Piggy May made the day even more memorable by whispering hoarsely, 'I've heard there's 180,000 of 'em ashore. I make that about 180 each. What are you going to do with your lot, then, Jan?" (*ibid.*, p.190.)

Humour lay in perception, often the difference between reality and appearance. A twisting of perception made a place or situation ridiculous. In middle age Causley found himself back in the Far East despite his wartime observation that he would never return. He found himself in Bugis Street in Singapore, a street famous for its transvestites.

Causley and his friends sat at a table to watch the girls, who were alluringly dressed and, no doubt, for sale. They paraded on high heels and smiled at the men at the table.

> The painted glance that fails to hide,
>   Somehow, a terrible innocence.

('Bugis Street', *CP*, p.337 v.3 l.7, v.4.)

Then the shock of revelation:

And for a dollar Singapore
Photographs of the girls.
But they
Are boys.

(*ibid.*, v.4.)

The shock of revelation comes despite all the images of war that throng the poem. Causley still has the capacity to be shocked; the experience of war in the Far East years earlier has not diminished his innocence:

A pedlar blocks our path;
Reads every word I do not say,
Pushes an orchid dunked in gold
Across the dirty tablecloth
And my hand shakes, but not with cold.

(*ibid.*, v.5.)

The theme of innocence and experience is one that Causley was to return to throughout his life. He was influenced by his readings of the poems of William Blake as well as A. E. Housman. Above all he observed his colleagues in the Navy, some wicked and corrupt, others moral and upstanding, a few downright mad. He was fascinated by the moral choices that war imposed on the individual and many of his poems were to be shot through with the images and metaphors of war.

'The Navy is also, of course, nothing if not a great habitation of wild eccentrics and weird individualists, some of whom, regrettably, would almost certainly be locked securely away from the rest of society on land. The degree of tolerance afforded by messmate to messmate seemed to me as admirable as it was sensible.' (*Hands to Dance and Skylark*, p.182.)

Most of these individuals were quite as normal as Causley himself.

'If there is such a creature as an average sailor, then my observation is that he is more than likely to be a man particularly steadfast and faithful in his love; and he longs for the stability and security of home. (*ibid.*, p.182.)

Others are cut from stranger cloth:

'One Leading Seaman I knew refused to leave the ship on his own account at all points between Greenock and Perth, Western Australia, on the simple grounds that he did not like foreigners.' (*ibid.*, p.182.)

Causley saw this man being marched up and down the quay in Alexandria and Colombo under armed guard. The Navy would not tolerate such a weird form of individuality and put him ashore 'for his own good.'

There were men of even stranger mien:

'What happened, finally, I sometimes wonder, to the remarkable P., who would sit for a whole evening placidly embroidering cushion-covers, then suddenly hurl his handiwork in all directions and in a series of mad rushes, attempt to walk up the sides of the mess-deck? His ambition, he once told me with perfect seriousness, was to be the first human being to walk upside-down, with no aids other than his own two feet, on a ceiling.' (*ibid.*, p.183.)

There were the two sailors who lived like an old married couple. Causley refers to them as Y and Z. Y constantly rescued Z from danger, particularly from his (Z's) violent mood swings. From time to time Z would dress up in an extraordinary collection of exotic and somewhat effeminate clothes:

'He would pad about in a gleaming scarlet silk dressing-gown embroidered with golden dragons, a yellow satin mandarin's cap, and a pair of elegant silver sandals. Sometimes his get-up would include a fez, ballooning green Turkish pants, and high, red-leather boots: puffing away, meanwhile, at a foul-smelling selection of cigars and cigarettes (most of them years old, tinder-dry with age, and flaring dangerously) he had gathered in ports from Lisbon to Singapore and Hong Kong and back. Nobody raised an eyebrow as this extraordinary figure flitted about in our midst.' (*ibid.*, p.185.)

To emphasise the utter weirdness of this couple Causley quoted Y's reassuring words to him:

'And then, pursuing a train of thought I found difficult to follow: 'I gotta good mind to take up religion. Make a nice change from Pitman's bloody short-'and.'' (*ibid.*, p.186.)

The utter lack of self-consciousness in these characters conveyed a sort of innocence in Causley's eyes. They were very good at what they did, they were telegraphers, and fully accepted by their mates for what they were. Causley was keen to observe them without judging them, realising that he himself must have appeared strange to many of his mates.

In his observations he had much material for the short stories he would soon set out to write. There were harmless men and there were men who were nothing short of dangerous, vicious and criminal. Causley tended to avoid these men at all costs.

After the Japanese surrender at Rabaul Causley had to serve out his time in the Navy before the demobilisation that would inevitably come. He was fascinated by the Far East and determined to learn what he could of it. Convinced that he would never have the opportunity to return, he took mental notes on many of the places he visited and later used them in short stories and poems.

Writing about his early diaries in 1979 Causley felt very much distanced from them:

'For the first three years of my life in the Navy, I kept a diary: not of my movements, but of my immediate personal reactions to the various situations in which I found myself. I had the vague idea that it might form a useful, factual basis of a book – of poems or prose, or both – I might one day write. When, finally, I was demobilised and arrived home from the Pacific laden not only with the debris of my kit but also a sack of Australian canned fruit, I wrapped the journals in a small, brown-paper parcel and stored them in the back of a wardrobe.

On two or three occasions during the years that followed, I untied the string, releasing the sour, damp odours of the past, and tried to read the journals again. But always, after a few pages, I put them away in a mood of utter depression. They are written by a man I scarcely know; are about a reality I have long lost touch with: or so it seems to me. They spoke of fears, loves, hatreds, jealousies I had long forgotten, and of characters and situations I can now barely identify. Disconcertingly, too, I saw a man who – had he been a painter – had his eye too close to his subject, his nose too near the canvas.' (*ibid.*, p.190-191.)

Causley had to make a break from the Navy and the war before he would be able to write about his experiences with anything approaching objectivity. To appeal to a reader who had not been there he could not afford to appear too indulgent in his memories. He would indulge in a touch of nostalgia from time to time but often in a self-mocking way that he was usually able to contain. He was a very private man who could not reveal too much of himself in his writing, not because he had anything to hide but in order not to stand in the way of his themes.

Despite his fear and loathing of the sea and his dread of such grim places as Devonport Causley had developed a strange love relationship

Petty Officer Causley with cap at jaunty angle on H.M.S. Glory, 1945.

(Special Collections Library, Exeter University.)

with the Navy. As a writer he found much material in what he had observed in his six long years in the senior service. He had also gained the confidence to rise above the ranks of clerical assistants; as a petty officer he had been responsible for the smooth functioning and well being of a number of subordinates. In the diaries of his early years in the Navy he only made one reference to telling subordinates what to do. He was quite proud of the 'bollicking' he had to give. He was now ready for the next stage of his life. The Navy had been good to him; he had been sent to a shore base and then to a large ship, he had only limited time on HMS Eclipse and on HMS Marigold, a corvette based in Gibraltar, he had been sensibly promoted and had found his niche in wartime service.

On his return to civilian life he knew what he would do. There was no question of leaving Cornwall for long; he would continue to support his mother in Launceston. He would write plays, short stories and poems for publication and return to a life of hard work, music, drama and the companionship of close friends. He would mourn the friends who had been killed during the war, men like Eric Sullock and Rattler Morgan would never be forgotten.

He had, to some extent, learned patience and a certain amount of tolerance in the Navy. He had found his primary vocation confirmed, writing would hopefully play a large part in his future life. His other vocation, a challenging one by all accounts, was to be teaching.

Before leaving the antipodes Causley and another sailor were entertained for several days by a very hospitable and generous Australian couple who showed the men around and indulged them with motoring trips to the Blue Mountains and around Sydney. They fed them well and the rather spare Causley must have gained a few pounds before the long sea journey home. In his kit bag Causley carried his diaries and the gift from his hosts of the sack of Australian canned fruit, no doubt for his mother in Launceston.

He brought other baggage home with him. In his poem 'Nursery Rhyme of Innocence and Experience' Causley wonders if the gifts he has brought home are relevant:

O where is the sailor
  With bold red hair?
And what is that volley
  On the bright air?

O where are the other
　　Girls and boys?
And why have you brought me
　　Children's toys?

('Nursery Rhyme of Innocence and Experience,' *CP*, p.4 vv.14-15.)

On one level Causley shows us how his old pre-war self is dead and that what he brings or sends to post-war Britain is possibly irrelevant. He has fulfilled his promise but what now has he left to offer? Of what relevance are his six years in the Navy when it comes to making a contribution to society and earning a living? Has he become institutionalised and unable now to move with the times? He even wonders if his choice of career is possible.

With his usual lack of sentimentality or self pity Causley wonders if life is passing him by. The long awaited anti-climax of the end of his service career gives pause for thought.

In a slightly later poem 'Yelverton' Causley reconciles himself to what might have happened:

Here, by the church of battleship grey,
　　The auctioneers' advertisements, and the sound of water,
Among the lovely ponies and the fat golfers
　　I met her by the Rifle Range.

And so, when peace came, I never returned to Glasgow.
　　Now I work as a fitter in the dockyard
And, I might say, as an ex-service man
　　I was lucky to get the job.

We've a nice little place here at Yelverton,
　　And although it's a bit chilly in the winter
There's plenty of room on the moor for the kiddies
　　And we have nice little outings to Princetown.

All the same, I am sure you will see
　　Why I do not wish to join the Rifle Club?
Myself, on the long winter evening,
　　I find myself thinking of the Royal Naval Barracks at
Devonport.

('Yelverton', *CP*, p.26.)

This wistful poem shows one of Causley's ways of dealing with change and insecurity; irony that can sometimes blossom into sarcasm. Here Causley shows us, in the common language of everyday people, what could have happened to him as an ordinary working class sailor after the war. He lists the things that are anathema to him: marriage to a woman 'with a voice like a loudhailer,' working 'as a fitter in the dock-yard,' 'a nice little place here at Yelverton' (a rather bleak village on the edge of Dartmoor), and 'nice little outings to Princetown' (an even bleaker village on the moor dominated by its huge prison).

Soon after Causley arrived home his medals came by post in a small cardboard box. There were four of them[22] and he put them back in their box and kept them with his Uncle Lewis' two Great War medals in his desk. He never had them mounted on a bar to wear at Remembrance Day services.

There was one piece of wartime baggage that would have the power to transform Causley's future life; his future opportunities to write poems and short stories and the possibility of having them published.

---

22 Pacific Star, 1939-45 Star, Defence Medal, 1939-45 War Medal.

Thirty Years in Chalk Siberias

Causley kept a dairy for four years and wrote the occasional biographical piece[23] in middle age; apart from these revelations there is very little material on his life. But all is not lost; far from it.

In old age he constantly and patiently told friends and scholars who asked him about his life: 'It's all in the poems.' He was not trying to be evasive, merely expressing the truth of a man who had his ego well in check. We turn to his poems not only to find out where he was at the time and what he was doing but also to put the meanings in the context of his life. Fortunately for us, Causley placed his collected poems in roughly chronological order.

In 1946 Causley and the Navy parted company after six years. He sailed back to Blighty's shore to be demobilised, hand in his kit and be fitted for his Burton suit. He returned home by train to Launceston; from now on he would have to pay for his own railway tickets. He was entitled to fifty-six days paid leave, time to decide his future.

> And they say:
> 'You must be fed up with your leave,
> Fifty-six days is a long time,
> You'll start work before it's over –
> You'll be tired of nothing to do,
> Nothing to think of,
> Nothing to write about.
> Yes: you'll go back to the office
> Soon.'

('Demobilisation Leave,' *CP*, p.19 v.6.)

---

23 Michael Williams (ed), *Both Sides of Tamar,* 1975, pp.5-16; Charles Causley, *Hands to Dance and Skylark,* 1979, pp.7-11 and 164-191; Harry Chambers (ed), *Causley at 70,* 1987, pp.94-104 and 106-111.

Back in his comfortable home at 23 Tredydan Road with his beloved mother Causley could have drifted back to his tedious clerical job. Even if his old job were no longer available he could have found a similar post in Launceston where he was known and trusted. He would have gone back to playing the piano, going to church, swimming in the baths and enjoying a pint in The Bell or The White Hart. He would even have taken his mother's pekinese Wang for short walks. Life would have been sweet and undemanding, a reward for six years of service in various mainly hot parts of the Empire.

The Causley who left Launceston in 1940 with twelve other recruits on the Plymouth train was not the Causley who walked into 23 Tredydan Road in his 1946 demob suit and a suitcase full of Far Eastern souvenirs and Australian canned fruit. He was more confident and more ambitious, even with his moments of profound doubt. The Navy had taught him that he had far more to offer than an ability to keep accounts. He had done sufficient travelling for the time being; his memory was full of images that would remain with him for a very long time. If written down they would remain fresh forever.

Taking advantage of a government scheme designed to help returning servicemen and the English school system after the 1944 Education Act, Causley enrolled in a teacher training programme. He would study for a Cert. Ed. in teaching at primary and secondary level, specialising in English and History. Maths would always be problematical but it was a difficulty to be overcome.

He eventually heard that he had gained a place at Peterborough Teacher Training College beginning in the Autumn Term of 1947. Knowing little about the East Midlands and the Fens he did his research and set off to begin his course as a mature student a good ten years older than many of the freshmen beginning the course.

His poem 'Autobiography' shows him on the cusp of his new life as a student, still missing the places he had visited in the tropics and somewhat gloomily trying to adapt to the reality of a wet English summer and an unknown future:

Now that my sea-going self-possession wavers …
… But the English Sunday, monstrous as India, shivers,
And the voice of the muezzin is the voice of the station announcer.

The wet fields blot the bitterness of the cry,
And I turn from the tactful friend to the candid sky.

('Autobiography,' CP, p.21.)

Once in digs in Peterborough Causley soon settled down to studying the art and craft of teaching. He would be one of the new teachers of the immediate post war who would be given the task of raising the standards of national education in the post 1944 Education Act era.

When not on teaching practice, reading dense books on the theory of education or writing essays, Causley visited places around the rather drab city of Peterborough. The cathedral is undoubtedly the most glorious building in Peterborough with its uniquely surviving flat Norman wooden roof and interesting monuments to a queen and a giant. Writing was still uppermost in Causley's consciousness and he often found himself in a rather morbid frame of mind in flat grey country far from his native Cornwall.

His poem 'A Ballad for Katharine of Aragon,' set in Peterborough, contrasts the late queen and his dead friend Jumper Cross, both victims of man's inhumanity to man. Queen Katharine was divorced by Henry VIII after eighteen years of marriage and sent to a nunnery for the remaining three years of her life and Jumper Cross killed in the Italian mountains at twenty-seven and a half by a six-inch shell.

As I walked down by the river
Down by the frozen fen
I saw the grey cathedral
With the eyes of a child of ten.
O the railway arch is smoky
As the Flying Scot goes by
And but for the Education Act
Go Jumper Cross and I.

('A Ballad for Katharine of Aragon,' CP, p.2 v.1.)

This is a sad poem that shows Causley at the lowest point of homesickness and self doubt. He thinks about suicide:

O shall I leap in the river
And knock upon paradise door
For a gunner of twenty-seven and a half
And a queen of twenty-four?
From the almond tree by the river
I watch the sky with a groan,
For Jumper and Kate are always out late
And I lie here alone.

(ibid., v.6.)

Not only was Causley still mourning friends killed in the war but he was beginning to realise that he was nearly thirty and had no great prospects of marriage. He makes clear in the verse preceding the verse quoted above that:

Now I like a Spanish party
And many O many's the day
I have watched them swim as the night came dim
In Algeciras Bay.

(ibid., v.5.)

'Party' being the Cornish dialect word for a girl, a 'bit of stuff,' makes clear to the reader that the poet would choose to lie down with the young queen rather than the soldier!

The mood of despair reminds us of Causley's disastrously unpleasant voyage from Scapa Flow to Sierra Leone on HMS Eclipse. In the penultimate verse of the last verse 'For Jumper and Kate are always out late' we see a flash of humour that shows that, even in the depths of despair, there is something to be redeemed.

It is quite possible that Causley's black mood at the time was responsible for one of his rare mistakes. He was never at home with numbers; he mistook the dates that Katharine was queen (1509 – 1533) for the dates of her lifespan (1485 – 1536). As a result the line 'And a queen of twenty-four' should have been 'And a queen of fifty-one,' ruining the link between Katharine and Jumper Cross who was ' … a gunner of twenty-seven and a half' who probably would not have been wildly attracted to older women. Causley was a poet not a mathematician.

Such moods of despair were rare and Causley, though still haunted by the memory of dead friends and places to where he would probably never return, soon adjusted to Peterborough, classrooms of little 'oiks,' flat countryside, frozen fens and post war austerity. He visited the grave of a man whose life was even bleaker than his temporary self-imposed exile in the Fens after buying a second hand volume of John Clare's poetry in Peterborough market on a Saturday morning.

He had always had a great admiration for John Clare,[24] the farm labourer poet who was considered mad by most people. When Causley found his grave in 'the scythed churchyard' he was encouraged by the inscription 'A poet is born not made.' The landscape was still predominantly grey but there was hope:

And the poetry bursting like a diamond bomb

('At the Grave of John Clare,' *CP*, p.22 v.3)

And:

O Clare! Your poetry clear, translucent
As your lovely name,
I salute you with tears.

(*ibid.*, v.4.)

At the age of thirty Causley left the frozen fens and grey skies of the Soke of Peterborough with his teaching qualification. He was delighted to be interviewed for a post at his old school, the National School, off St Thomas Road in Launceston. The outcome was entirely favourable; he was offered the job by Rodney Keast, the headmaster, and by the governors. A point in his favour was that he could play the piano for assemblies and music lessons. He would join Mr Keast and Miss Trethewey to teach one of the three large classes that made up the National School that catered for the poorest part of Launceston. At first he taught a class of fourteen and fifteen year old pupils. Before long the secondary modern school opened and Causley chose to teach younger children of primary school age.

He moved happily back to Tredydan Road and settled down to a

---

24 John Clare, 1793 – 1864, was the son of a Northamptonshire farm labourer. He was an outstanding self-educated poet who died in a lunatic asylum.

quiet life of lesson preparation and getting to know his pupils. Coming back to teach in one's home town is always a challenge as well as a privilege. Causley knew a lot of his pupils' parents and grandparents and he took his job seriously. He joined the National Union of Teachers and remained a card carrying member all through his teaching career. Life wasn't always easy for him; mastering the art and craft of teaching was demanding. Living with a mother who had spent the last five years without him and had to reconcile the changes in him could not have always been straightforward.

His strengths as a teacher were patience, thoroughness, firmness and, above all fairness. He used his great sense of humour to defuse tense situations and often made up rhyming couplets to act as mnemonics. When he saw a child yawn in his classroom he sometimes said:

'I thought I saw the Severn Tunnel
Gazing at me like a funnel.'[25]

The child would be corrected but not humiliated. Causley could raise his voice but he kept his temper, and above all his sarcastic tongue, in check by the propensity for self-control learned in the Navy. He could be formidable but his occasional outbursts were always short lived and often resulted in an apology to the individual whom he had targeted. He did not teach by fear but by wise instruction and by example, often admitting that he had done something wrong. Unusually for the time he never used any form of corporal punishment.

He made a point of learning everything about an individual pupil's background and had a huge empathy for children from a similar background to his own. Demanding honesty he despised pretentiousness and arrogance. His sympathy for the individual did not make him soft but encouraged him to give the child the confidence he or she may have lacked.

One case in point was David Werran, a Cornish boy who had moved to Launceston from London in 1948. Apart from finding himself with rough children, he first heard children swear at the National School, he had recently lost his mother and was devastated, consequently his schoolwork suffered from a lack of application. With the Eleven Plus exam looming Causley took David aside and talked to him, explaining how he had lost his father at an even more tender age. He encouraged

---

25 Supplied by Mrs Les Baker.

him to study for the exam and gave him sympathy and confidence. As a result David took and passed the Eleven Plus and went on to do very well. Now semi-retired after a distinguished career as an advisor to various governments he lives in Launceston, just down the road from the old Grammar School. He still has his reports from 1949 from the National School with their signed comments in Causley's neat and careful handwriting. From what he says one gets the clear impression that, like Causley, he received his best education at the National School.

Causley's classroom was large, high up under the roof and looked out onto the sloping valley of Harper's Lake, the turbulent stream that used to rise up and join with the Kensey to flood Causley's birthplace near St Thomas' church a few hundred yards downhill. The steep green fields gave onto numerous allotments below the school, the stream threading its way down the hill at the valley's bottom. It was an inspiring view, entirely rural at the steep town's edge.

Although establishing himself in Launceston as a good teacher Causley was also writing plays, short stories and poems. His progress as a writer would be from plays to short stories to poems with later return to drama. One of his best known later poems is 'Timothy Winters,' a description of a typical small boy from a very deprived background. When asked in later life if Timothy was based on a real boy Causley vehemently replied: 'Yes, by God he was, poor little devil!'

Although Timothy existed the length and breadth of the country of post war austerity there are clues that he is local to the Westcountry. Suez Street smacks of Plymouth with its service emphasis:

He lives in a house on Suez Street

('Timothy Winters,' *CP*, p. 65 v.4.)

And,

And his missus ran off with a bombardier

(*ibid.*, v.5.)

The use of the word 'helves,' a Cornu-English word referring to the noise a cow makes when deprived of her calf, puts Timothy also firmly in Launceston. In fact Causley had a lad named Brian Martin in mind when he wrote 'Timothy Winters.' Brian lived in great poverty in Tower

Street in Launceston in one of the ancient picturesque slums that were demolished in the 1960s to make way for council flats. He was infested with lice and his arms and legs were covered in scabs and sores. When Brian wrote a story and read it aloud to the class the children laughed and made fun of him. This made Causley very cross and he gave the class a lesson in humility, telling them that everyone had something to offer. He gave another pupil, William Sleep, as an example of someone who had a great imagination.

Causley was an egalitarian, a teacher who deliberately had no favourites. He was a disciplinarian who respected his pupils: 'Children, you walk among them at your peril.' (letter to Susan Hill.)

Consequently he never talked down to them or patronised them. His history lessons were particularly inspired, often memorable. His enthusiasm for telling and illustrating stories came to the fore and he held classes enraptured by his passion. Much of this approach to history comes out in his poem 'In the Willow Gardens,' written for children but just as suitable for adults. One can imagine the view from Causley's classroom windows over the allotments commonly known as the 'Willy Gardens' by generations of National School pupils including young Causley:

But in the Willow Gardens
I don't hear Tom nor Jack,
But I can hear the huntsmen
Along the forest track
All through the Willow Gardens
I see them riding plain,
The iron knights of Normandy
And Robert of Mortain.

(*Figgie Hobbin*, p.62 v.3.)

Music lessons were also popular; Causley played the piano in a lively manner and often gave songs that he was teaching to the class a local flavour. He had a fine singing voice and passed on his great enthusiasm for music and folk songs to his class. His love of folk songs was to influence many of his future poems.

Causley's egalitarian philosophy meant that he was opposed to the withdrawal from class of pupils with special needs. He was happy to differentiate in his classroom to the extent that he would teach children who were 'slow' or, in the jargon of the day, 'educationally sub normal.' He believed in inclusion rather than teaching these children in a separate class. In his classroom they received plenty of help and encouragement; their presence was good for the other children in the class and they were never made to feel inadequate. Causley firmly believed that everyone had something unique to say.

Like any teacher Causley made enemies. A Launceston lady who wishes to remain anonymous once told Causley that she was teaching her daughter to read. Causley replied that she should know that was his job and that she should leave it to him. Perhaps she was making a mess of it. The lady said to me: 'I never said another word to that Mr Causley again, not as long as he lived.' Causley certainly took his job seriously.

We can see something of Causley's view of the unique nature of children with special needs in his poem 'Healing a Lunatic Boy.' It is a difficult poem, the gist of it being that when a boy considered mad was 'healed' he became ordinary and lost his unique view of the world that had sustained him. The point, however, is that this is just one boy. Causley was not against helping pupils who had problems. Each case was different and had to be carefully considered on its merits. All pupils were to be treated separately in the same room, not lumped together in a special unit.

Seize my smashed world
Wrap it away.

('Healing the Lunatic Boy,' *CP*, p.97 v.5.)

Perhaps Causley had the 'mad' John Clare in mind when he wrote this poem. Had Clare been treated for his condition and 'made normal' he would have been made incapable of describing his unique vision of the world.

Causley got on very well with Mr Keast, even agreeing to become Honorary Treasurer of the football club that played at the weekend on Priory Field, almost opposite Causley's home in Tredydan Road. He must have been well out of his comfort zone; participation in any form of team game was anathema to him as was any form of mathematics. He was willing to give it a try and took it seriously, such was his respect for Mr Keast, even though he readily admitted that 'he did not know one end of a football pitch from the other.'

His relationship with Mr Toy, headmaster of Launceston College,

Charles Causley, who was dubbed the Poet Laureate of Cornwall.

(Photo by Irving of Exeter. Courtesy of by Nick Irving.)

the grammar school, was quite different. Harold Spencer Toy, himself an ex Launceston Grammar School boy, who was to later become a Cornwall County Councillor, had served as an officer in the Camel Corps in the Middle East and was considered arrogant and overbearing by Causley. Causley disliked the fact that parents were never welcome at the Grammar School. Toy became his bête noir, riding a high framed bicycle around town 'two feet above criticism.' David Werran shared this view; when he came to leave the Grammar School he received a bad reference from Mr Toy which he felt was unmerited. So he proceeded to tear it up and Causley wrote him a reference which he considered much fairer. Causley was prepared to take risks when his sense of justice was offended. When talking to David he referred to Toy as 'insufferable' and 'that despicable man.' David was one of the few Launceston College pupils of the time to go to university. He considers the school in the 1950s to have been a poor grammar school.

Every morning Causley left the house in Tredydan Road to walk up Wooda Lane past a row of slate built houses to the National School a few hundred yards away. He dressed smartly in jacket and collar and tie, his shoes polished and his hair neatly combed. After a busy day in the classroom he came home downhill in the late afternoon with marking and preparation to be done before writing poems and short stories in the evenings or occasionally going out to play the piano in the Brotherhood Hall, the former YMCA building slightly uphill from the National School. His life had taken on a satisfying quiet rhythm with his mother and numerous friends for company. There was no need for him to keep a diary because he found plenty to write about in his poems.

He was happy to settle back to life in Launceston and was always ambivalent about his home town, having a healthy scepticism about town politics and entrenched attitudes. He was very much a part of the life of the town but part of him was elsewhere. In 'On Launceston Castle,' one of his most brilliant poems, written in 1980 especially for an anthology of Westcountry writings to help with the restoration of Exeter Cathedral, he writes:

> But once I was too young
> And still am too unsure
> To cast a meaning from
> The town's hard metaphor.

('On Launceston Castle,' *CP*, p.286 v.6.)

The memories of his wartime postings continued to haunt him along with the regret that he would probably never travel again. The life of the imagination pressed on his sensitive nature like a sweet wound.

A Life on the Brown

Once firmly established back in Launceston Causley had a few individual poems published in such periodicals as *West Country Magazine*, edited by fellow Cornishman J. C. Trewin, and *Poetry Quarterly*, which printed his poem 'Homage to Louis McNeice' in its Autumn 1947 edition. He had written a number of poems in his head and on scraps of paper on board ship towards the end of the war as well as memorised the ideas for a collection of short stories.

In 1948 Muller published another of his one act plays ten years after bringing out *Benedict*. *How Pleasant to Know Mrs Lear* was a Victorian piece about three sisters who lived under the thumb of their domineering mother Mrs Lear. They were named Melody, Britannia and Hepzibah Lear and were looked after by a stage struck Cornish maid named Salome Perkins who was outspoken to the point of insolence. Her rudeness was tolerated by the sisters because it expressed opposition to their mother. The theme of women's emancipation runs through the play with numerous references to the enlightened works of John Stuart Mill and Charles Darwin. There are comic scenes that rely on suspense and timing and the dreaded Mrs Lear never actually appears, although she can be heard approaching and retreating from the front door before running off with Mr Ratazzi, a widower and bad church organist. Ironically the three sisters are liberated by their termagant and repressive mother.

This light-hearted play reveals Causley's coming to terms with living with his mother again. He was in no ways suggesting any direct similarity between his mother and Mrs Lear; if he identifies with any of the characters it is the cheeky maid constantly misquoting Shakespeare while longing to be on the stage. All is made right by the wealthy sister of Mrs Lear who also lived in dread of the matriarch and who will now send Salome to drama school (and elocution lessons).

In 1948 Laura Causley was sixty-one years old and, while by no means an old lady, she depended on her son for emotional and financial security. Causley would no more have cast her out on the world than he would have put the family cat in the gas oven. He had a keen sense of duty and was very fond of his mother. They could not have always got on well together; they were too similar in temperament, too easily annoyed and irritated by trivial things. They clearly loved each other but it must have been hard for Causley to come to terms with the fact that he would probably look after his mother for the rest of her life. This would have diminished his marriage prospects and called into question his sexuality in the eyes of some of his friends and acquaintances. Years later the gay scholar and writer A. L. Rowse[26] (whom Causley now had come to dislike) said to Causley: "So, you're one of us … ," to which Causley replied: "Yes, that's right, a Cornishman." It is quite possible that Rowse, who had a definite cruel streak, was trying to embarrass Causley, having picked up on his repugnance of homosexuality.

An interesting footnote to *How Pleasant to Know Mrs Lear* was the choice of the name Hepzibah, a reference to his Aunt Hephzibah who died tragically young of diphtheria in Newton Abbot at the height of Queen Victoria's long reign.

Near the beginning of the play Hepzibah says some lines of verse which establish her character as repressed and resentful:

O the blackthorn and the wild cherry
And the owl in the rotting oak tree,
Are part of the Cornish landscape:
Which is more than can be said for me.

In his slightly later poem 'Able Seaman Hodge Remembers Ceylon' (*CP*, p.29.) Causley used the same lines, minus the comma and colon, in the first verse. He was still unsettled by his return to civilian life and missed some of the exotic places he had recently visited. Here we have a unique example of self plagiarism, of Causley recycling a good verse and a crossover from his drama to his poetry.

The name 'Lear' also brings us back to Victorian times. Edward Lear[27] was a reclusive painter and poet who suffered secretly from epilepsy. Because he could predict when a fit was coming on he made sure

---

26 A. L. (Alfred Leslie) Rowse, 1903 – 1997, was a brilliant Cornish historian, academic and poet known for his arrogance and irascibility.

27 Edward Lear, 1812 – 1888, was a British artist, writer, poet and traveller who popularised the limerick and nonsense poems.

to suffer in private and his secret was safe from the public and from Queen Victoria whom he tutored in painting. A noted painter of birds and landscapes he is much better known today for his nonsense poetry and his early use of the limerick for comic effect. Causley identified with him: he wrote amusing poems for children, he loved to travel and he was very fond of cats. He illustrated his own collections of poems and, like Causley at this point, wondered if he would ever earn any recognition for his poetry. Much of his poetry contains a sweet melancholy that very much appealed to Causley.

The problem, for Causley, was finding a publisher for a relatively unknown poet in the dark days of post war austerity. Fortunately an American lady living in Kent by the name of Erica Marx[28] had decided to make new poetry affordable. In 1941 she founded the Hand and Flower Press to publish new poets at prices that most people could afford. Her 'Poems in Pamphlet' came out at 1/- apiece and each featured the work of a single poet.

Causley's first published collection of poems was *Farewell, Aggie Weston!* which came out as Number 1 of 15 in the 1951 series. 'Aggie Weston' refers to The Dame Agnes Weston Sailors' Home in Plymouth, established for the physical and moral well-being of mariners. There are twenty-eight poems in the collection; most are about the Navy. 'Chief Petty Officer,' 'Song of the Dying Gunner' and 'Nursery Rhyme of Innocence and Experience' first appeared in this slim but beautifully designed and printed book.

Other poets featured in Erica Marx's *Poets in Pamphlet* were never heard from again. Among them were Marx herself and such luminaries as the hymn writer F. Pratt-Green. Causley was easily the best and most successful poet introduced to the reading public by this admirable series of affordable collections.

1951 was also the year that Carroll and Nicholson published *Hands to Dance*, Causley's only collection of short stories. Once more the dominant theme was life in the Navy with all its absurdities and hilarities. Clearly Causley was on his way to becoming a noticed new writer and poet.

In 1952 he was nominated a bard of the Gorsedd Kernow (the Cornish Gorseth) and took the bardic name 'Morvath,' the Cornish for seabird. Causley wore the blue robe a few times but, while acknowledging

---

28 Erica Marx, 1909 – 1969, was a Jewish-American poet who published books and pamphlets in Paris and Kent before retiring to a houseboat.

that he had been paid a great honour, could spare neither the time nor the enthusiasm to travel all over the granite kingdom to various Gorsedd events. Although he was sometimes a clubbable man he often lacked the time and inclination to commit himself to regular and predictable events. In later years he became a Freemason; his robes that still hang in a cupboard in his house at Cyprus Well show remarkably little wear. Freemasonry was an enormous power in the land in North Cornwall. Centred around Tintagel and the Arthurian and Holy Grail legends, it was very popular after the war.

It is probably at this time that Causley took out a mortgage on 23 Tredydan Road. He was doing well at the National School and becoming established in Launceston. To provide security for his mother and himself he therefore took the prudent opportunity of putting his money into bricks and mortar. His future was opening up; he was in his middle thirties, fit and healthy. His writing gave his powerful imagination the opportunity to transcend and develop his small town background; being published twice in the same year by two different publishers gave him the recognition he deserved and the confidence to continue writing, especially poetry.

At around this time he gave up smoking, an activity he had enjoyed but also felt a little guilty about. The only reference to his smoking occurs in a very early poem 'At the Grave of John Clare':

And smoking a pipe on the gate
At Maxey Crossing,
I thought of the dead poet:

('At the Grave of John Clare,' *CP*, p.2 v.2.)

His mother probably was partly instrumental in his giving up smoking. She continued to go to her beloved WI and to live quietly and mostly contentedly in the town in which she had lived all of her adult life. Causley said very little about her; she was very much a part of his private life and was only occasionally referred to in his poems, and then mainly after her death in 1971. He referred to her as 'that indomitable lady' in later broadcasts. She must have told him a lot about 'Lanson' and the North Cornish countryside providing him with the roots he could never have put down in Devon, his father's county. For some reason Causley invariably referred to the county in conversation as 'Devonshire' rather than the more colloquial 'Devon.'

For example she told him about the wandering entertainer with the dancing bear who knocked on the door of St Stephen's School one hot Thursday afternoon towards the end of Queen Victoria's reign, when Laura Bartlett was a pupil there. She had also shown young Charles around the seaside town of Teignmouth, in Devon, where she had worked in service and met her husband. She made a point of pointing out the house where Keats spent the summer and autumn of 1818 looking after his brother Thomas who was dying of tuberculosis. The result of these two memories are Causley's poems 'My Mother saw a Dancing Bear' and the very early 'Keats at Teignmouth, Spring 1818.'

Until the end of his life Causley spoke with a soft north Cornish accent that denoted Launceston to anyone who hailed from the area. His attempts to suppress the pronounced Westcountry 'r' were often unsuccessful. He was never self conscious; what he had to say was of far more importance than how it was said. He was Cornish through and through but never a 'professional Cornishman.' He had nothing but contempt for poseurs who traded on their Cornishness.

He thoroughly enjoyed teaching the sometimes rough Launceston children. At first he read them prescribed poems such as 'Winnie the Pooh' which both he and his classes found dull and insipid. One Thursday afternoon he had a double class of older children and brought in the wrong book. He was reluctant to leave sixty potential trouble-makers, even for the two minutes that it would have taken to find the 'right' book. So he opened the book and started to read a mediaeval ballad to the restless class. The combination of the ballad and Causley's obvious enthusiasm for it caught the attention and the imagination of the class. He never looked back; he even wrote poems and jingles for his class from that point on.

Causley always considered his teaching role to be a privilege. He often said that he didn't know how much he had taught his pupils but that they had taught him 'an awful lot.' He found his pupils totally honest as well as brave. Feeling that he did not have the sympathy of one young lad he said to him: "You don't like me very much, do you?" The boy replied: "No, I don't." Causley reckoned that it must have taken a lot of courage to come out with such a frank reply to an adult in a position of responsibility.

When Causley wrote poetry for children he didn't write down to them. He soon realised that children experience love, death, and betrayal and accept them in an even more direct way than adults. He pulled no punches; from the very first he wrote poems that were to be read equally by children and adults. His poems were very successful and popular; he became probably the most eminent children's poet of the twentieth century. Poems written exclusively for children he considered condescending, mere 'jingles.' He refused to patronise children because in them he saw a directness and a frank acceptance of the world as it was.

He continued to write his poems in his head before writing down drafts which he would ruthlessly edit. His hand written drafts were full of crossings out, additions and subtractions and, when completed, carefully typed out. A poem that would yield all its meaning on a first reading could never be a good poem. Repeated readings of the simplest poem would yield meanings and associations that would continue to develop on further readings. An example of this is the third verse of 'My Young Man's a Cornishman':

> He plays the rugby football game
>   On Saturday afternoon,
> And we shall walk on Wilsey Down
>   Under the bouncing moon.

> ('My Young Man's a Cornishman,' CP, p.221 v.3.)

The form of this verse is very simple. The third line implies that the young man, having enjoyed himself in the afternoon would always be there in the evening to spend time with his girl. The 'bouncing moon' implies a memory of the game of rugby which was shared by the lovers.

Because Causley was a good musician, having played the piano semi-professionally, learned the violin at school and the tin whistle in the Navy, his poetry contains a lot of music. The rhythms in many of his works make putting them to music difficult and often superfluous. The mediaeval ballad form lends itself to Causley in a natural way. Although Causley is known primarily as a writer of ballads the majority of his poems are not ballads. It is possible that the poems in the ballad form are the easiest to memorise and, therefore, to go back to. The internal rhymes of the third lines of some verses give the poems a rhythm that makes them often bright and clear. Despite the form many of Causley's poems are dark. He describes children as often leading lives that are 'mediaeval' and instinctively close to the mysteries of life and its betrayals and tragedies. They can share and understand sadness and have an acceptance of reality often absent in adults. Children tell the truth and expect it in return.

When Causley was a young man before the war he tended to look eastwards towards London rather than west into Cornwall. He saw the capital as a place of enablement and opportunity. He would have happily left the office in Launceston to starve in a London attic and write. After the war he realised that inspiration did not lie in a distant place but in where he was at the time. He said that if he had gone to live in London he would have never written a thing. His town of around four thousand souls was all the inspiration he needed. To this he added his memories of distant places and a nostalgia that was seldom sentimental. Like all good poets he could not just sit down in front of a blank piece of paper with a blank mind. His poems formed in his head and were committed to paper when they were ready.

'Unlike a river or stream, a work of the imagination derives rarely from a single source. To describe the texts in this exhibition as 'Launceston' poems, therefore, may be a little misleading. In a very real sense, each poem I have ever tried to write is a 'Launceston' poem. Wherever we are, here or at the other side of the world, each of us carries a past, a present and intimations of the future as part of the body's luggage.' (Charles Causley, Introduction to *The Spirit of Launceston*, 1994.)

Many of Causley's early poems are haunted by images of the Navy and of war. They are a form of exorcism of a completed part of his life. In his old age Causley said that he had learned how to write poetry in his head in the Navy. He also said that the only favour that Adolf Hitler had done him was to get him out of the office in Launceston. He also noted impressions and unusual words down on scraps of paper that he stowed in his kitbag.

In 'The Seasons in North Cornwall' Causley constantly uses sea-going analogies to express each of the four seasons. In a short poem of four verses he uses nine nautical images to good effect to enhance the features of each of the seasons. The last verse is the strangest and most memorable, a perfect verse of poetry:

My room is a bright glass cabin,
    All Cornwall thunders at my door,
And the white ships of winter lie
    In the sea-roads of the moor.

('The Seasons in North Cornwall,' *CP*, p.31 v.4.)

In this verse Causley combines the two things he dreaded the most. He hated the damp cold of a Cornish winter with its lack of brightness and its short days and he often loathed the sea. In his poems there are numerous and varied examples of his dread of the sea and its destructive power. In a late poem, 'Morwenstow,' the last verse sums up a lifetime's fear:

> When will you rest, sea?
>> When moon and sun
> Ride only fields of salt water
>> And the land is gone.

('Morwenstow,' *CP*, p.392 v.5.)

In an earlier children's poem 'Ramhead and Dodman' Causley expresses the same bleak outcome. Ramhead (Rame Head) and Dodman Point are two headlands on the south coast of Cornwall:

> 'And never O never
>> In cold or heat
> Old Ramhead and Dodman
>> Together will meet.'

> But softly the sea
>> As it chanted their rhyme
> Said, "I'll swallow the pair of you
>> All in good time."

('Ramhead and Dodman,' *Figgie Hobbin*, p.48 vv.4-5.)

Joining the Navy and going to sea had been a 'romantic mistake' for Causley. It did, however, give him the opportunity to get to know his enemy.

His first and only book of short stories *Hands to Dance*, later republished in 1979 as *Hands to Dance and Skylark* with a biographical introduction about his time in the Navy, contains a collection of strange and often ironic tales mainly about the Navy, but a few are set in Launceston. One of the best as well as most unusual, 'Mrs Lisboa' (*Hands to Dance and Skylark*, p.91.), marks a transition from Gibraltar to Launceston. It is a story with a gruesome surprise which is mentioned casually in the last sentence and shows Causley's good sense of suspense and timing that he used to good effect in his short plays.

But poetry, and later poetic drama, was to be his real forte. It soon became a habit and an obsession. If the poem he was writing was not going particularly well Causley would go out for a walk, often along Under Lane past the swimming baths, out into the country where hills rose on either side of the fields that lay beside the Kensey which flowed down from Bodmin Moor to curve round the steep castle hill to meet the wider Tamar on its strong southern surge to the sea at Plymouth. He saw this river as an analogy of life, going through different stages before gathering strength but losing identity before eventually merging with the salt water of the wild and dangerous ocean.

Causley was comforted by the truth. He hated evasions and obfuscations, preferring to face unpleasant facts rather than to conceal them or brush them aside. Religion often occupied his thoughts. He didn't call himself a Christian or a churchman, comparing himself with Dr Johnson who seldom entered a church but always took off his hat in recognition when passing one. Undoubtedly he was a Christian but he would have considered himself a rather unworthy and disorganised one. He was fond of church services, church music and of the theatrical rituals of the 'high church,' but he didn't pretend to be overtly religious, preferring not to discuss the matter. Religion was one of the rare subjects on which Causley was evasive. He would have hated people to see him as 'worthy' or certain of his own salvation. His God was a very personal one; very real but hard to attain and to be approached on a very personal level. Causley was never to be pinned down as an Anglican or a Methodist. He described himself as 'vaguely low church at one time'; he maintained an open mind and often doubted mankind's ability to live up to God's offer of salvation.

As he grew older Causley loved to visit churches. Among his favourites in Cornwall were the magnificent granite church of St Nonna at Altarnun, beside Bodmin Moor, known as 'the cathedral of the Moor.' In its graveyard are some examples of the work of Nevil Northey Burnard, the brilliant self taught and mentally unstable stone carver. Other favourite churches were St Neot with its wonderful mediaeval stained glass windows linked to the Cornish Mystery Plays and its oak branch mounted on the tower, isolated Warleggan, where the eccentric parson sometimes locked the church door and preached to cardboard cut-outs and, above all, the twisted and flamboyantly Anglo-Catholic St Pratt's at Blisland. As an old man Causley would quietly sit in an ancient Cornish church for many minutes either alone or with a valued friend. Whether he prayed, meditated, thought or looked at the ceiling or screen would be impossible to say. He probably did all of these things as well as composing poems in his head or repeating and refining lines of verse.

Causley never searched for subjects for his poems. The subject matter had to come to him, had to knock, or even 'thunder' at his door. It was only allowed in after careful consideration and after thoroughly brushing its feet on the doormat. It then waited in the parlour for a while before being asked to come into the writing room with the piano and painting of Nelson on the wall and be committed to blank paper before numerous crossings out and additions. 'A poem is never finished only put aside' was Causley's view.

He believed that a poet had to stick at it, to get down to it. The composition of poetry became such a passion that he felt guilty when he wasn't working on a poem. Even when he was reading his poems aloud to audiences in middle age or broadcasting on *Poetry Please* or *Desert Island Discs* a part of Causley would rather have been writing poetry. Everywhere he went Causley carried a little notebook and a pencil to jot down ideas, words or whole lines of verse.

In his thirties the centre of Causley's world no longer lay east of Launceston nor completely west in Cornwall. Inspiration came from all four quarters of the globe as well as from 'under his nose.' Exposure to the wider world had shown Causley that there was no one place, no Mount Parnassus, where poetic inspiration was to be found. Without his firm roots in Launceston he would not have become the poet accessible even to people who know nothing of Cornwall. From the very start he was never just a local or regional poet, he was a 'Cousin Jack,'[29] a poet, a Cornishman who saw the wide world as his stage and all human activity as his inspiration. As he grew older he cast his net wider like a spider that drew all sorts of stories, experiences and historical incidents into his domain.

With the creation of a Secondary Modern School in Launceston the older boys and girls left the National School to the children of Primary School age. Causley chose to specialise in teaching younger children with their love of truth and vivid imaginations. He filled his classroom with folk songs, local and classical legends and stories. If a place didn't have a

---

29 'Cousin Jacks' are Cornishmen living and working away from Cornwall. It is not a pejorative term. Expatriate Cornishwomen are sometimes called 'Cousin Jennies.'

legend or a story and Causley believed it should have he often made one up. An example of this was Dockacre House, a rambling sixteenth century house in Launceston. It should have been haunted after the death of Elizabeth Herle, whose husband Nicholas confined her to a room in the house in the early years of the eighteenth century until she allegedly died of starvation, neglect or shooting by her husband's hand. Her monument, now hidden behind the organ pipes in St Mary Magdalene's church, states:

'Depart ye life ye December 1714 by starvation or other unlawful means.'

Causley wrote a poem about the man who haunted the house ('Dockacre,' *CP*, p.140.) and today Dockacre House is Launceston's famous haunted house. Someone once asked Causley if a particular local legend was actually true. He replied that indeed it was; he had made it up himself that very morning.

Poetic truth could, in a way, be subjective or objective. Literal truth took second place to allegorical truth. Parables were stories which contained truth in the moral rather than exact historical sense. Taking the Bible as the prime example of the dangers of an entirely literal interpretation we can see Causley's reluctance to be pinned down on the subject of religion. His unusual poem 'Ballad of the Bread Man' (*CP*, p.154.) is unequivocal in man's rejection of God's offer of salvation. It does not work as well as many of his other poems because it is didactic and uses somewhat trendy contemporary images.

Much of the 'meaning' of a poem or story lies in what the listener or reader brings to it. Causley was hardly ever didactic about the 'meaning' he put into a poem. He firmly believed that a good poem raised far more questions than it answered. As Causley wrote in old age:

'In reading a poem, it's important to remember that there is more to the piece than that which lies on the page. To use a currently popular phrase, there is invariably a hidden agenda. Whatever its apparent subject, in the final count a poem is usually also about something else. The reader must be alert to suggestions, hints, intimations in the text. What, specifically, is said may be as relevant as what, specifically, is unsaid. The 'meaning,' that sometimes bothersome element, remains something entirely personal to the individual reader.' (Introduction, *The Spirit of Launceston*.)

In 1953 Causley's second collection of poems, *Survivor's Leave*, was published by Hand and Flower Press of Aldington in Kent. Causley dedicated the collection to Erica Marx. It was to be his last book of poems published by Erica Marx; her task in introducing Causley to the public was complete and Causley tacitly marked this in his dedication. Many of the poems were about the Navy and the war but the shadow cast by Causley's six years' service was beginning to lift, although it never entirely left him. Ms Marx was soon to move to a houseboat on the Kent marshes before dying relatively young in 1969. She remained a shadowy figure whose place in history will be recognised as an enabler rather than as an outstanding poet in her own right.

In 1954 Causley was awarded a Travel Scholarship by the Society of Authors. He was delighted by the award, which gave him the chance to get away from Launceston, if only to examine the town from the outside once again. Always pleased by recognition of his poetry Causley never chased the honours that would be regularly bestowed on him for the rest of his life. He travelled to several European countries in his long summer holiday from school.

A move to the publisher Rupert Hart-Davis[30] in 1957 resulted in the publication of a new collection entitled *Union Street*, more poems on a naval theme and even more set in Launceston and at school. Hart-Davis was a publisher who insisted on the highest standards of writing and design. He tended to choose books that he liked rather than those that would sell the most copies. Causley liked his integrity and found a wider audience through Hart-Davis. The 'Union Street' of the collection's title anchors it to the Navy and underpins a move towards 'civvy street.' Most of Causley's wartime demons were now exorcised although they would return from time to time to haunt him in middle and old age. Union Street in Plymouth is still a depressingly rough street of bars and clubs, a transitionary fleshpot connecting Plymouth with the rougher part of Devonport. It is famous for prostitution, fights and revelling matelots. It has a kind of rough tarnished beauty, a raffish air of seedy adventure and an atmosphere of carnal unreality. The street is, in every way possible, the opposite of Dame Agnes Weston's Seamen's Mission.

In *Union Street* we find the first of Causley's 'religious' poems. In them he brings the same questioning perspective that we see in his war poems. They are rarely didactic and raise far more questions than are answered. It seems that Causley's emphasis was changing from ships to churches. He had an ambiguous view of both; to Causley a ship was a floating community of men with a common purpose. Its enemies were

---

30 Sir Rupert Hart-Davis, 1907 – 1999, was a publisher who put the quality of the books he published above the amount of money he would make from them. He is the father of Adam Hart-Davis.

the wild and raving salt sea and German or Japanese aircraft, artillery or warships. A ship was an alarming and vulnerable entity that could carry one to foreign parts, take one back to a distant home or slip beneath the waves taking most of its crew to a cold death.

A church could also be a place of mixed function and doubt. Causley's image of a ship with three masts was becoming an ark, a building with a nave and many nautical associations. Like different ships individual churches could be attractive and take one on a journey with a secret destination. But others, like HMS Eclipse, were unpleasant and places of negativity; often Causley would enter a church to find nothing for him there. On the other hand certain churches meant a great deal to him; St Thomas' church which lies only yards from Causley's birthplace in Launceston was a particular inspiration as was the church of St Michael in Trusham. In later life Causley described himself as a 'church crawler' with a fascination for the ancient churches of Cornwall. It seems that familiarity with a particular church would develop into an acceptance and a fondness for the building. Nothing was straightforward in connection with Causley's relationship with the sea and ships, churches and religion.

The Royal Society of Literature made Causley a Fellow in 1958. Not only had he had three successful collections of poetry and a book of short stories published in six years but he had also served as a literary editor of the BBC radio magazines *Apollo in the West* and *Signature*. The performer in Causley was to find a good outlet in radio, increasingly so as he grew older.

After ten years as a teacher Causley was approaching the age of forty. He was settled, successful and mainly happy. He was growing close to his numerous friends both in Cornwall and the wider world.

Two poets who had a great influence on Causley were Louis MacNeice[31] and W. H. Auden.[32] Like HMS Glory, MacNeice came originally from Belfast; he died in 1963 before Causley had a chance to meet him. During the war Causley had read MacNeice's poetry and enjoyed it very much. He liked the raw quality of the verse and the uncompromising truth of his ideas.

The poet who showed Causley the purpose of poetry was Auden. Before the war Causley realised that Auden was warning his readers that

---

31 Louis MacNeice, 1907 – 1963, was a Northern Irish poet and playwright known for the realism and directness of his poetry.
32 W. H. (Wystan Hugh) Auden, 1907 – 1973, was an Anglo-American poet who grew up in England before becoming an American citizen. He alternated between traditional and modern poetic forms.

appeasement would fail and that Hitler's armies would ravage Europe in the same ways as the English Army savaged the Highlanders after the Battle of Culloden. Auden had also shown Causley the musical qualities of the ancient ballad form. Causley's development of that form gave many of his poems a musical quality that was later to make it difficult to set them successfully to music. Like Auden, Causley was a poet who celebrated place and universalised it.

Another poet who Causley had enjoyed since his young adulthood was Siegfried Sassoon.[33] By the time Causley was an established poet Sassoon was an old man who felt that his poetry had been forgotten and that he was only now remembered as the officer who rebelled against the senseless waste of the Great War, threw the ribbon of his Military Cross into the Mersey and initially refused to go back to the Front. Causley and Sassoon kept up a lively correspondence until the latter's death. They occasionally met and enjoyed each other's company.

Closer to home Causley continued to mourn his friends who had been killed in the war. He seemed to have some form of survivor's guilt, realising that most of his friends had experience a much harder war than he had. He kept in touch with the artist Stanley Simmonds with whom he had found much in common in Gibraltar. They were to remain firm friends for the rest of their lives and would meet from time to time, usually somewhere in Cornwall. After his retirement Simmonds and his wife Cynthia came to live in Cornwall and their friendship deepened to the extent that Cynthia was to call Causley's mother 'Mum' for the rest of her life. She also sent Laura postcards from travels all over the world. Most of the extended Causley family called Laura 'Aunt Causley,' showing a fond respect so typical of Cornish people. Simmonds painted a very fine portrait of Causley sitting in the sun near the back door of his house in 1987.

Within the granite kingdom[34] Causley became friends with Jack Clemo,[35] the blind poet of the china clay country, the 'High Country' north of St Austell. This industrial area is easily one of the strangest and grimmest parts of Cornwall; 'plain grey terraces of houses form grim

---

33 Siegfried Sassoon, 1886 – 1967, was an Anglo-Jewish poet and writer who, having won the Military Cross for bravery as a young officer in the Great War, turned against the war, famously throwing the ribbon of his award into the River Mersey before eventually returning to the trenches. His poetry helped to inform a generation of the horrors of war.

34 Causley frequently referred to Cornwall as the 'granite kingdom' rather than as a county or a duchy.

35 Jack (Reginald John) Clemo, 1916 – 1994, was a deaf and blind Cornish visionary poet with a strong Christian faith.

industrial villages surrounded by huge conical and mounded waste tips of white sand, a by product of the extraction of china clay by high pressure hoses. Brass bands and a great feeling of solidarity among the proud people who live in this area redeem the dour nature of the clay country environment.'

Clemo was a very religious man who inspired Causley with his stoicism and clear poetic vision. When he married he insisted on having Causley there in the chapel as his best man. Clemo's version of Christianity was uncompromising and interesting to Causley's enquiring mind.

Another distinguished clay country man was A. L. Rowse, a brilliant scholar, writer and poet. Causley counted Rowse among his friends. He had a Cornish working class background in common with him and wrote to him from HMS Glory at the end of the war explaining that he very much admired Rowse's determination to transcend his environment and pursue an academic career. He told Rowse that his example had caused him to rise above his menial clerical job and apply for teacher training after the end of hostilities.

Causley could never share Rowse's occasional contempt for the common man and the working class. He disliked Rowse's tendency to rant, plainly evident in his autobiography *A Cornish Childhood* and such poems as 'Homecoming to Cornwall: December 1942.' The venom Rowse reserved for his working class family and for ordinary people in general would sometimes bubble to the surface when he returned to the place of his birth. Causley found this trait unattractive and repulsive. He admired Rowse for his persistence, scholarship and erudition but not for what he perceived as a lack of humanity. Perhaps he saw traits in Rowse's character that he himself could have developed had he been a more arrogant man.

Rowse's love-hate relationship with Cornwall was a far more exaggerated form of Causley's ambivalence. Causley being the more humane man expressed only the occasional irritation to close friends. He had even been known to say 'I hate this bloody place!' when finding the bank had closed before he arrived at the door. His sense of humour allowed him to laugh at himself in a way that the far more insecure Rowse was unable to do. Rowse described himself as being 'hopelessly Cornish.' Causley was definitely a more hopeful Cornishman.

In 1957 Causley was asked to prepare an anthology of verse from the Westcountry, entitled *Peninsula,* by MacDonald Publishers in London. Causley chose poems by natives such as Jack Clemo and relative but perceptive outsiders like John Betjeman.[36] When it came to Rowse Causley included a Rowseian rant and the statement about his being 'hopelessly Cornish.' Rowse found Cornwall full of people he considered stupid and unenlightened, including members of his own family. One of the things that bothered him was that in Cornwall he could not be openly gay as he was in Oxford. He was, however, drawn to Cornwall and ended his days near St Austell. Despite his rants he was kind to his mother and considerate to his housekeeper. He reserved much of his occasional venom for his few faithful friends, among whom Causley could not be included in his old age.

This first anthology gives a good indication of who many of his friends were at the time. He didn't choose poems because they had been written by friends; the standard of good verse had to be met, but the poets had to be accessible to the anthologer. In the Westcountry in general and Cornwall in particular a network of writers and poets existed as it does today.

If Rowse represented to Causley what he could have become Betjeman stood for a melding of the London literary world that Causley, as a young man, had considered so important and the Cornwall he knew and loved. One of Causley's earliest and most poignant poems 'Song of the Dying Gunner AA1' (*CP*, p.6.) was dedicated to Betjeman in *Farewell, Aggie Weston*, the 1951 Hand and Flower edition. For some reason this dedication was removed in later collections.

Betjeman was a firm friend of Causley's. Both men shared an offbeat sense of humour, both men were performers, Betjeman to a greater extent than Causley, whose television appearances were rare. When Betjeman was a young man in London he recognised the eminent politician Sir John Simon, who he considered stuffy. In the middle of Oxford Street the young Betjeman threw himself onto the pavement in front of Simon and faked a convincing epileptic seizure. As he foamed and thrashed on the ground Simon sidestepped him and continued on his unperturbed way.

Causley never did anything quite as outrageous. However, it is captured on film that he jumped fully clothed into a swimming pool during a school swimming gala in Launceston, an unusual thing for a teacher to do, but typical of Causley's offbeat approach to teaching. No doubt his young pupils learned that day that one cannot take oneself too seriously.

---

36 Sir John Betjeman, 1906 – 1984, was a very popular Poet Laureate, broadcaster and defender of Victorian architecture with a deep love of Cornwall.

Betjeman shared a passion for old churches with Causley. He is buried in the churchyard of 'Sinking Neddy,' the isolated church of St Enedoc. His tombstone is much more flamboyant than Causley's and fully reflects Betjeman's mainly extrovert nature. Both men had a secretive side and they got on well together over the years. Causley was later to develop even closer friends, Ted Hughes[37] being the best known.

In 1955 Causley wrote a strange but fond poem, 'Betjeman, 1984.' He depicted the ageing Betjeman, now almost seventy-eight, living in an oppressive Orwellian world in which all antique architecture and objects had been removed. It concludes with a harassed but defiant Betjeman remembering:

> Lord, but how much beauty was there
> Back in 1955!

('Betjeman, 1984,' *CP*, p.75 v.5.)

Ironically Betjeman was confined to a wheelchair by 1984 and died during the course of that year. It would be easy to assume that Causley had written the poem in that year; a more careful second reading of it would deepen the meaning and establish the true context.

As time passed Causley's poetry developed and changed. Occasionally he would look back to an earlier poem and dislike it, eventually he would regard all the poems he had written as works in progress. But we, the readers, would not distinguish any change in the quality of his poetry in the nearly fifty years that he was writing it. Causley's range of subjects would increase and the complexity of his poetry would inspire many valid interpretations and possible answers to the questions raised.

There were transitions in Causley's poetic forms. The early ballads gave way to elegies and later to more imagist poetry. In the 1980s Causley travelled widely and adopted a more modernist style with forays into blank verse. He did not suddenly change from one form to another, there were many reversions to earlier forms. His children's poetry did not mirror his changes in form; the claims that Causley's poetry is 'accessible' ignores the layers of association and meaning that increase on further readings. Also conveniently ignored is Causley's gift for letting the reader draw their own conclusions.

---

37 Ted (Edward James) Hughes, 1930 – 1998, succeeded Sir John Betjeman as Poet Laureate in 1984. He was an outstanding poet who was born in Yorkshire and settled in North Devon after the suicide of his first wife Sylvia Plath.

SIBARD'S WELL

After many years at Tredydan Road, Causley and his mother decided to move house. It was 1952 and Causley was in his mid thirties. They would look to buy a larger house with a different outlook; the idea of the National School looming across the park between the Causleys' little house and the bulk of the castle and the upper part of the town had become a little oppressive. Causley needed a quieter house in which to write, a house away from the rush of the trains behind the house and the traffic grinding up the hill on its way to the town centre.

A suitable house, 2 Cyprus Well, was found on Ridgegrove Hill, a steep lane leading out of town on the opposite side of the castle hill. It was a Victorian mid-terrace house quite unlike its neighbours on either side. It was a secret house with a front door and one window giving onto the steep, narrow hill descending into the valley on the other side of town from Tredydan Road. It had much in common with the old house: it was snug, not far from the town centre and had a delightful walk out into the countryside downhill from the front door. It was to become the house associated most with Causley's productive life and work. There is a plaque on the house by the Kensey where Causley was born, but Cyprus Well most encapsulates Causley's place in the world. At present it has no plaque because it stands empty. The Causley Trust, supported by the Causley Society, plans to make it into a study centre and residence for writers. Once more it will come into its own.

Causley bought the house and soon he and Laura made the move over the hill. The house suited them both very well; each could have their own sitting room and bedroom with plenty of room both inside the house and in the garden at the back.

The house had a limited aspect from the front door and the solitary window onto a steep overgrown bank directly across the narrow hill. The main aspect of the house lay to the rear. The front door opened into a tiny lobby where coats were hung, shoes and sticks kept a step down from the sloping pavement outside. A narrow door opened into a snug parlour with two comfortable armchairs and a fireplace and mantelpiece. An interior window gave onto a small kitchen with a small bathroom beyond in an outshot.

Through a door on the left steep stairs ascended to the first floor. Opposite this door was another leading to another sitting room with a window onto the garden, unobscured by the outshot. On the back wall was Causley's piano and round the walls bookcases held many of his books. A desk provided plenty of space for writing. This was Causley's inner sanctum; he must have blessed the absence of a window onto Ridgegrove Hill. Here he could write undisturbed, looking out of the window onto the garden from time to time and playing the piano when the mood took him.

Upstairs Laura Causley had the larger bedroom on the right and Causley the smaller room on the left. Both rooms were light and airy with windows in both directions. There was even a tiny box room for the storage of books and the keeping of accounts.

Back down the stairs a door led directly into a small conservatory with kitchen and bathroom leading off it. A glass paned door with coloured square panes in the corners, a feature typical of this part of north Cornwall, led to a level area paved roughly with Delabole slate with a small cherry tree by the wall and a bottlebrush shrub near the door. There was a wooden bench to sit on and comparative privacy between the stone walls at the two sides of the property. A black painted wooden wicket gate led a few steps down to a wilder garden area overhung by a large cypress tree. From here a small back gate led to an alley that went back to Ridgegrove Hill. It was a snug house, a winter house, generally warm except in the isolated and uninsulated little bathroom in the outshot. Causley had grown up with baths in a tin tub in front of the kitchen fire so he accepted the relative frigidity of the bathroom without much ado.

From the front door a sharp short climb past the leaning stone garden wall of Dockacre House leads to the curved and level Dockacre Road, running at right angles to Ridgegrove Hill. Crossing this slightly dangerous road one climbs the even steeper Angel Hill to arrive somewhat breathlessly beside the Southgate Arch that leads to the winding streets of Launceston town centre. The Causleys did not have so far to walk to the centre of town as they had from Tredydan Road. Causley could vary the route of his walk to the National School; he could walk along Dockacre Road as it curved to become Wooda Road. Beyond the Passmore Edwards Institute the road went downhill for a couple of hundred yards to cross busy St Thomas Road and arrive at the National School crouching just below the brow of the hill. He could equally have taken a sloping alley from the far corner of Dockacre House which led to a level parade ground adjacent to St Mary Magdalene's churchyard from where he would have walked into the town centre past the recumbent statue of Mary Magdalene on the church's east wall. No doubt he would have flicked a pebble up onto St Mary's granite flank from time to time *en passant*.

Turning one's back on the churchyard and looking between the lime trees on the parade ground's edge one can look down on the long and wavy roof of Dockacre House. Beyond, at right angles and at a lower level, can be seen the slate roof and outshot wing of Cyprus Well. On a dark day the remote slopes of Dartmoor, miles away in 'Devonshire,' can look like a far mountain rampart when lit by the watery slanting rays of the sun.

Angel Hill and Ridgegrove Hill once formed the main packhorse route from Launceston on its steep hill down to Polson Bridge on the River Tamar and England a couple of miles away. The names on this side of Launceston are predominantly Saxon, Cyprus Well being a corruption of the Saxon Lord Sibard's well. On the Newport side of town many of the names are Cornish and look to points further west.

From the front door of Cyprus Well a left hand turn would have taken Causley on one of his favourite walks, one comparable to a long wander from Tredydan Road past the stone walled Jubilee Bath along rural Under Lane. Down steep Ridgegrove Hill past a couple of houses on the left and a small quarry on the right he would have crossed two small railway bridges that crossed the former metals of the Great Western and Southern Railways[38] as they arrived from England to Launceston. Then round a bend to cross the River Kensey which had curved round the castle hill in its winding journey to the Tamar and the Channel. The house at Cyprus Well was about the same distance from the Kensey as the house at the end of Tredydan Road. Beyond the shaded stream the lane coiled round ancient Ridgegrove Mill before joining Ridgegrove Road at right angles. A right hand turn along the Kensey valley led to

---

38 Both railways, combined at nationalisation, had long closed, leaving Launceston without any rail connection.

Polson Bridge and a left hand turn would lead eventually back to the Round House at Newport. It is a varied, rural and satisfying walk with views over field and woods, a peaceful perambulation suggestive of contemplation and much leaning on the parapets of bridges. A walk requiring a little effort and a certain amount of faith as to the outcome. It must have suited Causley very well.

Once settled in at Cyprus Well, with the boxes transported and unpacked, the Causleys settled in to a contented and productive life. Laura could walk up to the centre of town and her beloved Women's Institute and was mistress of the kitchen, with its red kitchen cabinet and electric cooker. Friends came regularly to visit, both adults and children. Boy Scouts came in April to work for bob-a-job. One young grammar school scholar in scout uniform had the job of dusting Causley's numerous books on his orderly bookshelves.[39] Relatives and friends came to the house and were given tea and biscuits and, on special occasions, scones with Cornish cream and strawberry jam.[40]

The Causleys obtained two cats, Kensey and Pinky. Kensey was a rather aristocratic Siamese cat with the usual slight disdainful squint of his race. Pinky was much more common, a Cornish moggie. They were safe on Ridgegrove Hill. There was not much traffic and only one door onto the road so both cats had the run of the small garden and the neighbours' gardens.

Parking was rather a problem. Causley had bought a car, a Morris Minor, that he drove around town, mainly in low gear. The car could be parked outside the house with one set of wheels on the narrow pavement, the handbrake firmly on and the car left in gear. After a while Causley rented a garage up the hill and along Dockacre Road at Prout's Corner, not far from the former upper town workhouse. Causley was never an enthusiastic driver and seldom ventured far from Cornwall. He was never very happy with mechanical devices and matters of a purely practical nature.

In 1957, six years after the publication of *Farewell, Aggie Weston!*, Causley's fourth collection of poems, *Union Street*, was published by Rupert Hart-Davis. The title reflected Causley's change of emphasis from wartime survivor's guilt to questions of a religious nature. Apart from the title poem 'Union Street' one of Causley's best known poems, 'The Ballad of Charlotte Dymond,' was included in this collection. It

---

39 Keith Brooke.
40 In Cornwall the jam is spread on the scone and the cream on the jam.

emphasised Causley's deep roots in Cornish history and legend and universalised a local story which is still mentioned and mulled over today.[41]

It would be a great mistake to think of Causley as just a Cornish or topographical poet. Nearly all his poems, whether written for adults or children, have a universal significance. This fact is borne out by the publication in 1958 of *Union Street* in Boston, Massachusetts by Houghton Mifflin. It is inconceivable that only Americans of Cornish extraction bought and appreciated Causley's poems. There were to be American editions of Causley's poems from time to time in the future.

Causley was also writing articles on Jack Clemo, the slightly older Cornish poet whose uncompromising and often deeply religious poetry profoundly interested him. Causley and Clemo shared a proud working class background and upbringing. Clemo's uncompromising religious ideas and striking poetry fascinated Causley who was to be best man at Clemo's wedding in the heart of the clay country.

Just before the Causleys moved to Cyprus Well Ted Hughes moved down to North Devon while retaining his London flat. With his deep love of nature and of the countryside and encouraged by his older brother Gerald, Hughes settled near North Tawton. Within a couple of years Hughes' wife Sylvia Plath committed suicide in their London flat. Six years later Hughes married his second wife Carol Orchard who was to outlive him after his early death from cancer in 1998. Hughes and Causley were to visit each other for the rest of Hughes' life. It is significant that Hughes' granite monument on the northern part of Dartmoor makes one think of 'Eden Rock,' Causley's late poem which he always placed last in his collected works.

During the settled 1960s Causley took his mother on trips abroad, often by coach. They went to Italy, visiting Rome, Florence and Pompeii. Laura kept a meticulous photographic record of their travels with notes on the backs of her photographs in a neat hand. A visit to Russia provided some fascinating snapshots. Causley looked far more relaxed in these informal photographs than he did in the later posed publicity shots, which were often taken by people he did not know. He had the knack of attracting local cats; photographs of him seated often included a cat on his lap. The record was three kittens in a row!

In the very early 1960s changes were happening in education that mainly appealed to Causley. As Christopher Milne[42] put it in the early

---

41 See Jane Nancarrow's excellent novel *Stones and Shadows,* published by Scryfa.

42 Christopher (Robin) Milne, 1920 – 1996, was the son of A. A. Milne, creator of *Winnie the Pooh*. He and his wife owned and ran The Harbour Bookshop in Dartmouth for years.

Laura Causley and friend at the back door of 2 Cyprus Well during the 1960s.

(Special Collections Library, Exeter University.)

1970s:

'Where children once sat in silent rows all working at the same task, now they all moved about each working at different tasks. Where once they learned with tears now they learned with pleasure. Where once schools were inward-looking, isolating themselves from the outside world, now they looked outwards, a part of that world; high windows with a view only of the sky were replaced by low windows with a view of the neighbourhood; walls and fences were lowered. Subject after subject fell to the conqueror. The elements of physics, chemistry and mechanics, previously taught only as specialist subjects only to older children, were now introduced to infant schools. Arithmetic became the New Mathematics. Multiplication tables were replaced by coloured rods. Foreign languages were spoken not written. Spelling and grammar took second place to poems and stories. History was how people lived, not dates of kings and Acts of Parliament. Geography, too, was how people lived, not exports and imports and principal rivers.' (Christopher Milne, *The Path Through the Trees*, p.189.)

Like all change in education, it was to be two steps forward and one back. Causley, while keeping what was best in more traditional education, welcomed some of the changes. He was glad that a more relevant range of reading and factual books were being attractively produced for children of Primary School age and that many of them were now available in the school libraries. The earlier and more formulaic series of children's fiction books were giving way to much more imaginative books such as Ted Hughes' *The Iron Man*. The safe and comfortable series of books about boarding school life, pony clubs and groups of children having adventures and twisting their ankles was giving way to books about real situations and subjects to excite the imagination.

Causley, with his deep sense of reality and allegory, was gradually seeing his way to writing poems for children. It would take a few more years for both his audience to be ready and for him to begin writing these wonderful poems. Eventually *Figgie Hobbin* would open his poetry to a whole new readership or 'target population' in the horrible educational jargon of the day. In the meantime the horrors of war were receding a little, although they were never to retreat far behind the lines.

If Causley had any regrets during this settled part of his life it was that he had very little opportunity to travel. His mother, while still in good health, was becoming an old lady and he looked after her well. He would never have abandoned her to take off for parts unknown during

the school holidays. When he was younger he had travelled quite extensively during the school holidays but that time of freedom was passing.
Referring to early post-war travels he wrote: 'After 1947, [I travelled]
from Dublin to Warsaw and Moscow; from East and West Berlin to
Naples; and, many times, to Spain.' It is interesting to see his passports;
renewed every ten years, the photographs are sometimes serious sometimes cheerful, his profession changing from 'teacher' to 'writer.'

The limitation of not abandoning his mother, however self
imposed, must sometimes have weighed on him; one of his friends
remarked at a conference that he was looking a little downcast, like
'someone who has a mother.' Laura Causley became eighty years old in
December 1967. Her formerly robust health was now beginning to fail
her. A stroke in 1966 'robbed her of all except speech and the ability to
feed herself with one hand – her left hand.' Her disability kept her
housebound except when Causley or a friend took her on short outing in
a car. She could no longer struggle up Ridgegrove Hill and Angel Hill
into town. Always a fiercely independent lady this total loss of mobility
and independence must have been very hard for her.

'My mother was a woman totally unused to relying on others. In
everything but the moral sense – a very important exception, I recognised then, as now – she relied very little on me.' (*Causley at 70*, p.106-
107.)

Causley was faced with an impossible choice: he could put his
mother in a nursing home or try to look after her himself. Most people
advised him to do the former; he was a teacher who had to continue
working and could not afford to retire on a very meagre pension to completely devote himself to the care of his mother. In this context he
quoted Oscar Wilde: 'All advice is bad, and good advice is absolutely
fatal.'

At this point of desperation an old school friend came forward and
quietly suggested to Causley that she look after Laura during the day
while he was at work.

'If ever a saint – I shall call her B – stood before me, it was then.
She was experienced in geriatric nursing. For nearly five years, she came
to the house five-and-a-half days a week; cooked, washed, cleaned; saw
to my mother's needs; fed the cats [Kensey and Pinkey]; remained resolutely cheerful and absolutely imperturbable and tactful in the face of the
battalions of major and minor disasters that accompany crippling illness
and old age. And she bustled off to re-enter the world of her own family

and her ex-merchant-seaman husband each day at four o'clock, when I got home from school.' (*ibid.*, p.107-108.)

It would be fairly easy to find out who this wonderful woman was. I was asked not to reveal her identity as a mark of respect for her memory and so I do not know her name. Even if I were accidentally to find it out I would never reveal it. Both the selfless help to friends and the insistence on anonymity are typically Cornish. Laura Causley grew up in a close-knit society and departed this world with that society unchanged. No doubt she had, on many occasions, helped friends in their hours of need.

Without blowing a trumpet Causley also made huge sacrifices. He knew that if he abandoned his mother he could never live with himself after her inevitable death. In a way he was repaying a debt to the mother who brought him up and worked all the hours of God's week to support him when young. So he devoted himself every day to spend time with his mother who talked at length about her family and relations.

'And so the family roles were reversed. My mother was now the child. I became her parents – both parents. Though they had both died before I was born, I came to know them – slowly, curiously – better than I ever had before.' (*ibid.*, p.108.)

Now in his early fifties Causley never took a holiday away from home for over five years. He devoted himself to his mother and his school teaching took him into another, no less demanding world for seven hours out of the twenty four. He found the uncompromising company of children stimulating and, for him, it provided the necessary balance for his survival. Undoubtedly he had never spent so much time thinking about other people.

A young mother from the house next door brought her baby to see Laura every day. This unselfish act helped preserve the balance for both Laura and her son. As her long life drew to a close and as she came 'so slowly to harbour' her intimations of mortality must have reminded Causley that one day he too would grow old and die.

'My mother's only cure – and it was painful to acknowledge it – was death. It was impossible, sometimes, to avoid the feeling that one was being tugged into the same grave.' (*ibid.*, p.110.)

Life was not dismal for them. Through listening to his mother's memories of family he gradually got to know them: her father Richard Bartlett, her Uncle Stanley who never came home from Canada, 'the family past, the tribal memories, long dark, suddenly glowed; burst into

Charles and Laura Causley on a wet day in Launceston early 1960s.

(Southgate Studios, Launceston.)

flame.' (*ibid.*, p.109.)

Causley was also getting to know his younger self, stimulated by his mother's memories. The conversations with his mother unlocked a flood of poems which are among his most personal and most moving.

'After the evening meal, I would sit and write for an hour. This was absolutely vital to me. I was at no time prevented from getting words down on paper.' (*ibid.*, p.109.)

Apart from a detailed re-evaluation of family Causley's five years of devotion concentrated his mind back on the subject of religion. Talking about his mother:

'Her simple, Christian faith never wavered. She never sought, consciously, to impose it on others; certainly not, since the statutory days of Sunday School, on me. I lost my faith in the Thirties; but, 20 years later, achieved the beginnings of a kind of recovery. At heart I knew that her faith was the same as mine. A forest, a church, an art gallery, a seascape, a concert-hall, a river valley, a theatre, an expanse of moorland, all these were in one important respect the same to us both: temples of the spirit in which life, and its creator, were to be reverenced. She loved a church service, and for 75 years had hardly missed one of a Sunday. On the other hand, my feeling was – still is – that of Emerson: 'I like the silent church before the service begins better than any preaching.' (*ibid.*, p.109.)

The above is probably Causley's most complete statement in prose of his view of religion. In his poems he often takes the part of the non-believer, plays 'Devil's advocate' in his complete empathy. It is interesting that the passage from which the last few quotations are taken was broadcast by Causley as a Lent talk in 1977, six years after Laura's death.

By 1971 Laura's fragile health was declining. Causley saw his own predicament in familiar terms: 'I felt like a man tossed on a bleak sea, who must not lose sight of the light on the shore.' (*ibid.*, p.110.) She had been patience itself but there was no going back. The devoted carer B fell ill herself and Laura developed complications that put her into the geriatric hospital. She was beginning to slip away and was beyond being the person Causley had known and loved so well. The veil came down and she died on 24th November 1971 'on a cold, quiet, sunny November afternoon' when Causley was aged fifty-four years and exactly three months. She did not die alone but we do not know if Causley was with her when she died; it is probable that he was because he would have remembered his father dying away from him in an upstairs room on the last day of 1924.

Charles Causley relaxing on a family visit to Trusham during the 1960s.

'I was assailed by two fears. Would her death, when it came, be with dignity? Would I be there? I was obsessed by the thought that, after having spent so many years at her side, I should leave her to die alone after all. But those saintly nurses and orderlies in that geriatric ward saw to it that this was not so.' (*ibid.*, p.111.)

She was buried in the large churchyard of St Thomas' church, less than two hundred yards from the house where her son had been born. Causley chose the epitaph on her gravestone which reads: 'Blessed are the pure in heart: for they *shall* see God.' The italics on the word 'shall' in the text of 'Slowly to Harbour,' but not on the epitaph, are Causley's and can be seen as a rare affirmation of faith in a Christian God.

The last five years of Laura's life had a great effect on Causley's poetry and the result bears out his belief that inspiration can come from close to home. Through talking to her and, above all, listening he knew and understood the older members of his family. The result was occasional late poems dotted about among travel poems and others. He never grouped his family poems together in the way that he was to carefully group his later Australian poems, written in the early 1980s. In his collected works they are well worth searching out and reading as a group.

They are: 'Silent Jack' (Uncle Lewis Causley) (*CP*, p.269.); 'Richard Bartlett' (Laura's father) (*ibid.*, p.279.); 'Dora' (Aunt Nora Causley) (*ibid.*, p.280.); 'Uncle Stan' (Uncle Stanley Bartlett) (*ibid.*, p.282.); 'Photograph' (grandmother Bartlett) (*ibid.*, p.379.); 'Family Feeling' (Uncle Alfred Bartlett) (*ibid.*, p.404); and 'Ancestors' (Aunt Maggie Causley) (*ibid.*, p.416.)

Distant memories of Causley's father are recalled in 'A Wedding Portrait' (*ibid.*, p.271.); 'Tavistock Goose Fair' (*ibid.*, p.274.); and 'To My Father' (*ibid.*, p.410.). As Causley grew older he was able to remember his father because he found that he was physically growing more like him, remembering that Charlie Causley was prematurely aged when he finally died.

Charlie Causley was an invisible presence in a number of other poems. In 'Keats at Teignmouth, Spring 1818,' which Causley always placed first in collections of his poems, his father's presence is felt.

In his breast lay death, the lover
  In his head, the nightingale.

('Keats at Teignmouth, Spring 1818,' *CP*, p.1 v.4.)

Obviously Causley is referring to the doomed Keats who spent the summer and autumn of 1818 in Teignmouth looking after his dying brother Thomas. It would have been impossible for Causley to think of Teignmouth without thinking of his father who worked there and where his mother and father met. Both Keats and Charlie Causley died of tuberculosis; Teignmouth can be seen as a place of parting. Laura had said a hurried goodbye to her favourite brother Stanley at Teignmouth station as he came by on the London train. It is possible that Charlie Causley had a poetic streak that he passed on to his son. This does, however, bring us to the realms of supposition.

Charlie Causley is very much present in 'Trusham.' Apart from the fact that his name is misspelt on the village war memorial his opinion would have been the same as that expressed by 'an old man shoulder-sacked against the rain' who asks, in a rather direct way, why Causley had never married and ensued the continuation of the family name. This old man, who was most likely an outspoken local farmer named Alfred Bates, made Causley think of his father when he spoke to him. The images of the Great War, initially suggested by the Trusham war memorial, are impossible to forget.

In Rattle Street the mud is Flanders-thick.

('Trusham,' *CP*, p.135 v.3.)

The old farmer, 'shoulder-sacked against the rain,' who familiarly addresses Causley on one of his visits to Trusham makes us think of Wilfred Owen's poem about a gas attack in the trenches 'Dulce et Decorum est.'

Bent double, like beggars under sacks,
Knock kneed, crouching like hags, we cursed through sludge.

But Causley's inability to marry would not scrape off like the mud. His heart could not be reset and he could not see himself marrying. There is a guilty feeling in this poem; opportunities had been lost and the family name would now 'go scat.' What would Charlie Causley have thought of that?

In a way Causley was becoming his father. Growing older he was living into the middle age that his father never reached. It was as if the two generations became closer through the experience of memory.

Poems about Laura, although very significant, are few, indirect, and far between. They almost all date from after her death, the exception being 'My Mother Saw a Dancing Bear' (*CP*, p.230.), a classic poem of innocence being modified by experience. When she was a girl in the village of Langore she walked regularly to school at St Stephen's on the hill opposite Launceston. One afternoon the initial delight caused by a captive bear being made to dance in the school playground gave way to sympathy for the bear that was obviously unhappy and mistreated. Children are very aware of exploitation and injustice. Innocence is not inevitably lost as a result of experience, it is often preserved or even enhanced. In his old age Causley could not read this poem without choking up.

The poem was written quite soon before Laura died and it represents Causley's departure into children's poetry, which, as we have seen, was usually to be equally suitable for adults. There is a little wooden carved bear on the mantelpiece of the front room at Cyprus Well that Causley would have glanced at from time to time.

Other poems about Laura Causley are (indirectly), 'Ten Types of Hospital Visitor' (*ibid.*, p.232.); 'Ward 14' (*ibid.*, p.261.); and 'Scenes from Childhood' (*ibid.*, p.396.). She is very much present with Causley's father in 'A Wedding Portrait' (*ibid.*, p.271.); 'Photograph' (*ibid.*, p.379.); and, always the last in the collection, 'Eden Rock' (*ibid.*, p.421.). The first two poems about Laura are about her decline in hospital, the last, 'Eden Rock,' brings the family together after death in a very ordinary picnic, probably on Dartmoor.

Causley had begun writing poems suitable for children soon after his mother's stroke. His collection *Underneath the Water*, published in 1968, take as title a playground rhyme that connects Causley's war experience with the world of children's reality and fantasy down by the River Kensey:

Underneath the water
Six feet deep
There lies Hitler
Fast asleep.

It was not a collection of children's poems but the idea had been planted.

Also in 1968 James Turner, a writer and poet who had come to live in Cornwall, asked Causley for a poem. Turner had succeeded Lady Cynthia Asquith as editor of the Pan 'Ghost Book' series and, while compiling *The Fourth Ghost Book*, asked a number of local writers to supply contributions. Both Causley and Denys Val Baker, a Welsh writer who settled in Cornwall and edited and produced the influential *Cornish Review*, sent in material; Causley's was a poem called 'A Local Haunting' (*CP*, p.142.) based on a true case from the late seventeenth century made famous by Daniel Defoe and revived by the Rev. Montague Summers in the early twentieth century. It deals with the Botathen Ghost, the wraith of Dorothy Dingley who consistently tried to stop a schoolboy crossing a particular field near Launceston. It is the only poem in the whole Pan *Ghost Book* series which ran from the late 1950s well into the 1980s. The name 'Dingley' continues in Launceston; a hall at the central Methodist church is named 'Dingley Hall.'

In 1970 *Figgie Hobbin*, the first and best known collection of children's poems was published, and was an immediate success. Produced by Macmillan, a publisher that Causley had not used before, in hardback, it was soon out in paperback from the same publisher, making Causley, an established and well respected poet, almost a household name. Already a prolific broadcaster Causley found his reputation greatly enhanced by the book.

Causley dedicated the book to Stanley and Cynthia Simmonds, his close artist friends. Some of the poems such as 'As I went down the Catwalk' (*Figgie Hobbin*, p.55.) and 'King Foo Foo' (*ibid.*, p.43.) are pure entertaining nonsense while others like 'What has happened to Lulu?' (*ibid.*, p.16.) and 'Who?' (*ibid.*, p.96.) are dark and haunting. Many of the poems are set in Launceston but a reader who has never been there can be as captivated as one who knows the town well. These poems are never sentimental but imaginative and intriguing. History plays a great part in many of them. 'In the Willow Gardens' (*ibid.*, p.62.), which, for some reason Causley omitted from the *Collected Poems*, is a wonderful bit of escapism. Causley describes the view from his classroom windows and daydreams about how the allotments were in the early Middle Ages when they formed part of a royal deer park. He describes two old allotment holders, Tom and Jack, who work their plots without realising the history of the patch of land on which they stand. They are ordinary people with no sense of history or poetic imagination. Unlike Causley they do not notice 'the iron knights of Normandy and Robert of Mortain' hunting hares, boars and deer through the park which had become the Willow Gardens. They go on digging potatoes and nailing up corrugated iron, feeling sorry for Causley who they consider 'maze as a brush' and suggest he go home because 'You'm looking whisht and pale.' There is a total lack of communication between Causley and the gardeners. Although the poem is light and humorous it makes the serious point that even the best poet will not reach everyone with his vision.

Ghosts feature in several poems. 'Colonel Fazackerley' (*ibid.*, p.50.) outwits a terrifying ghost in his house and in 'Millers End' (*ibid.*, p.81.) the ghost turns out to be Bill the garden boy rather than the sinister spectre-like old lady. Death figures large in 'Tom Bone' which contains quite horrific images like:

Tom Bone as you lie there
On your pillow of hair,

('Tom Bone,' *CP*, p.220 v.4.)

This delighted children with their love of ghost stories and sense of the macabre. Causley pulled no punches and, as usual, there is no talking down to children.

Some of the poems are poignant. The last poem 'Who?' describes the adult Causley observing his young self wandering through the fields beside the River Kensey. It is as if he is seeing a ghost who casts no shadow and does not see him until addressed. In my signed first edition of *Figgie Hobbin* Causley wrote on the first page:

'Inscribed for Evan: encourager, friend, with admiration & warm good wishes Charles Causley' and wrote, on the title page, the last verse of the very personal 'Who?':

Why does he move like a wraith by the water,
Soft as the thistledown on the breeze blown?
When I draw near him so that I may hear him,
Why does he say that his name is my own?

('Who?,' *CP*, p.231 v.4.)

Another enigmatic figure in *Figgie Hobbin* is the Reverend Robert Stephen Hawker, himself a good but not outstanding poet. When Hawker was a young student at Oxford he dressed up as a mermaid (known as 'merrymaids' in Cornwall) and splashed around on rocks at Bude. He did this for a week and quite a crowd gathered to see him comb his hair and sing in the sea. Having proved the gullibility of people in general and Methodists in particular he left the sea and later became the famous Anglo-Catholic Vicar of Morwenstow where, apart from retrieving and burying drowned mariners, he reintroduced Harvest Festival and Easter Vestry Meetings.

In this poem Causley makes one of his rare mistakes. He states that Hawker was already Vicar of Morwenstow when he entered the water in a merrymaid suit. He proves the point by stating:

> And with arms straight down by her sides she sang
> 'God Save our Gracious Queen.'

('The Merrymaid,' Figgie Hobbin, p.68 v.7.)

According to the Reverend Sabine Baring-Gould, in his biography of Hawker *The Vicar of Morwenstow:*

'At full moon in the July of 1825 or 1826, he [Hawker] swam or rowed out to a rock at some distance from the shore, plaited seaweed into a wig, which he threw over his head, so that it hung in lank streamers half-way down his back, enveloped his legs in an oilskin wrap, and, otherwise naked, sat on the rock, flashing the moon-beams about from a hand-mirror, and sang and screamed till attention was arrested.' (p.21)

Queen Victoria did not ascend the throne until 1837 so when Hawker sang the National Anthem it would not have been *God Save the Queen.*

'He therefore wound up the performance one night with an unmistakable "God save the King"' (*ibid.*, p.21.)

Figgie Hobbin contains one of Causley's best known children's poems 'I Saw A Jolly Hunter' (p.14.) in which a man out to shoot hares accidentally kills himself with his gun because of a lapse of attention. It is a dark subject treated in a light humorous way, ideal for the direct vision of a child. Poetic justice is served on a man out to kill for sport. Causley's sympathy for animals also comes out in 'A Fox came into my Garden' (*ibid.*, p.17.) and 'My Mother saw a Dancing Bear.' (*CP*, p.230.) His point is that one should treat animals just the same as one would wish to be treated by other humans, a Christian message if you like. In many of his children's poems Causley makes a clear point and avoids the disparate moral angles present in many of his exclusively adult poems.

After Laura's death on 24th November 1971 Causley was grief stricken but also liberated from a situation of irreversible decline. Naturally he missed his mother but, just as she was released from suffering, so he was released from responsibility and drudgery. He began to wear his hair a little longer and to dress a little more fashionably as photographs taken at this time show. As his period of mourning passed he realised that he was now free to travel again and to spread himself a little more. He looked younger than his fifty-four years and he began to see the new directions that his life was taking. Close friends were to become even more important and the new direction in which his poetry was going was due entirely to his increasingly close relationship with his mother in the last years before her death.

Causley's friend D. M. Thomas summed it up in his poem 'Visions,' written for the celebration of his sixty-fifth birthday:

> And you, although of late you wear
> Your hair longer, your years lightly, suits
> Suitable for jet-travel, therefore
> Are less often in Cornwall than I care for
> Drive all the deeper your dark roots
> Into its granite. You are still here.

One opportunity that now presented itself was a role at the University of Exeter. In the 1970s there were no universities or university colleges in Cornwall, so Causley went to Exeter, which was then less than an hour's drive away up the A30 from Launceston. Causley was invited to be unofficial writer-in residence at the university, during his sabbatical from teaching, by Professor Moelwyn Merchant, head of the English Department. According to Mick Gidley Exeter University at the time was 'tweedy, traditional, and class-bound.' Causley was none of these things and so approached his role in higher education with a certain amount of trepidation. He wondered initially how he would fit in and seemed to walk around the campus with a permanent look of surprise.

Professor Merchant was a poet in his own right and encouraged poetry among his students, the majority of whom he liked very much. He encouraged Causley to be available to those students who wished to show him what they had written. It was Mike Weaver, a lecturer in English and fellow Cornishman, who took Causley under his wing during the period of Causley's sabbatical. They shared a love of Cornish writers and poets and a broad Cornish sense of humour that could be incomprehensible in the staff room to many of the academics. Although Causley was in awe of the university milieu at first he gradually settled in to

Charles Causley on Launceston Castle Mound during the early 1970s.

(Special Collections Library, Exeter University.)

become a valued member of the department and one who, above all, had time for the students and their creative problems.

Work at Exeter introduced Causley to American literature and poetry through the input of Mike Weaver, Ronald Tamplin and Peter Quartermaine. The latter invited and arranged for the Australian poet Chris Wallace-Crabbe to spend part of the academic year at Exeter. Wallace-Crabbe and Causley became friends and, as a result, Causley was later to make several trips to Australia. The formerly rather stuffy atmosphere at Exeter was changing as the seventies gathered pace.

In 1974 Causley wrote an introduction to *Richard Hooker and Company*, a collection of poetry written by third year students selected by an editorial group chaired by Professor Merchant. In it he stated that poetry was the 'direct result' of 'natural, personal compulsion.'

Causley's introduction to American poetry may well have led him to write in blank verse. Although extremely well read in British and European poetry, Causley had not taken much notice of such American poets as Walt Whitman and Ezra Pound. Not having had the opportunity nor the inclination to attend university he eventually overcame his awe at being a part of Exeter University and took to it, always putting his students first and often giving up his lunch hours to help them and to listen to them. He only developed close friendships with a few academics, Ronald Tamplin and John Hurst being the foremost.

Back at home in Launceston, now that his mother was dead, he developed other skills. She had always been the cook in the house and now Causley discovered ready-made meals from the supermarkets. Never an enthusiastic chef, he became a great fan of frozen foods and, later on, Admiral's Pies. He enjoyed a glass of whisky from time to time but never became dependent on alcohol. He needed to keep a clear mind to write and remained at all times in control. Never manipulative, he was still good at keeping his own space clear when he needed it to be.

From the microcosm of his home life and his close relationship with his mother he began to make himself available to the macrocosm of the world he had left behind when demobilised from the Navy. With both service and domestic restraints lifted his life expanded all through his fifties and continued to do so until almost the end of his long life.

By 1975 it was time for a major collection of Causley's poems to be published. Macmillan brought out his selection *Collected Poems 1951 – 1975* in that year. His popularity had recently been enhanced by his careful editing of the *Penguin Modern Poets* series. In *Collected Poems* Causley had carefully selected the poems from each book that he considered the most important. He put a lot of thought and effort into his selection and placed them in roughly chronological order. He made a number of small changes such as, for reasons of his own, leaving out the dedication to John Betjeman in the early poem 'Song of the Dying Gunner AA1.'

Selections of his poetry had formerly been published as anthologies with one or two other poets. An example of this is *Penguin Modern Poets 3*, with George Baker and Martin Bell, published in 1962. Now it was time to take stock of almost a quarter of a century of published poetry and put together those that he wished to be remembered for.

He began the collection with 'Keats at Teignmouth, Spring 1818' and finished it with 'A Wedding Portrait.' Each poem, in its way, is indirectly autobiographical. As his friend Ronald Tamplin quotes in his excellent essay 'Causley's Poems First and Last'[43]: 'Make sure the first one is right, and the last, and don't worry about what's in between.' Tamplin says that this was 'jokey advice' but it also has its serious and practical side. Even the most serious subjects had to be kept in proportion, to Causley humour was always more than just an effort to get a laugh. In his slightly self-deprecating way Causley would turn a humorous remark against himself to universalise it.

The *Collected Poems 1951 – 1975* was also published in Boston, Massachusetts by Godine in 1975, and was to be Causley's third American publication. In the last few years he had written mostly poems for children and had published very little exclusively for adults. At this point of his writing career it is interesting to note that he had always gone his own sweet way. He was part of no modernist movement or school, nor was he a part of any traditionalist movement. The revival of the Cornish language interested him but he was not prepared to write in a language that would be hard to learn and in which expression would not have been natural to him. He was no jumper onto bandwagons, neither was he stuck in a past that required much academic effort and study in a direction that would not have felt right for him, neither was he a chaser after honours. He was, in his unselfconscious way, a true voice of Cornwall.

He was interested in the resurgence of a truly Cornish identity, being Cornish by birth, upbringing and culture. A letter from the Devonian writer Henry Williamson is addressed to 'The Cornish Chough'[44]; Causley's drama can be seen to have roots in the *Ordinalia*, the Cornish

---

43 Michael Hanke (ed), *Through the Granite Kingdom*, p.39.
44 Williamson's letter is on display at the Special Collections Library of the University of Exeter.

religious mystery plays of the Middle Ages. But not for him the militancy of the late twentieth century. He was where he wished to be and he wanted to keep it natural. One of the few references to Cornish nationalism is in his early poem 'Cornwall':

> ONE day, friend and stranger,
> The granite beast will rise
> Rubbing the salt sea from his hundred eyes
> Sleeping no longer.

('Cornwall,' CP, p.36 v.1.)

Causley did not see 'the granite beast' that he compared with Caliban becoming a power in the land.

> Sail away monster, leaving only ripples
> Written in water to tell of your journey.

(ibid., v.5.)

In 1975 the National School finally closed to be replaced by St Catherine's School, a newly built primary school on the other side of town. Causley realised that his teaching career was almost over. He was, however, promoted to deputy head of the new school, a job he did for four terms. It was a reward for nearly thirty years of good teaching and dedicated service to the children of Launceston, first, and Cornwall Education Authority, second. Increased administration and time away from the classroom did not appeal to him. He was happier in the classroom or taking groups safely around the countryside to look as such interesting antiquities as Dupath Well near Callington to the south of Launceston.

Causley retired from teaching in December 1976 at the comparatively early age of fifty-nine. He had completed almost 'thirty years in chalk Siberias.' Now he could concentrate completely on writing. He had an enhanced pension and a comfortable income from the royalties from his writing. Indeed he said that he could have lived frugally on the royalties from 'Timothy Winters' alone. We must take this statement with pinch of salt; Causley did live frugally and was no materialist. After his mother's death he spent little money on decoration or furniture in the house at Cyprus Well. If stranded on a desert island he would have chosen a piano above everything else.[45]

Around this time Causley was honoured by the town of Launceston. He became a freeman of the borough; the first man given the honour at the day's ceremony was Tom Sandercock, the first traffic warden in Britain. Secondly came Causley who, like Sandercock, was presented with a vellum scroll hand lettered by Stephen Childs, a local artist. He was touched by the honour bestowed on him by his town. After the reception he asked Arthur Wills to come home with him and gave him a signed copy of one of his books of poetry to mark the occasion.

Another honour was the painting of a full length portrait of Causley standing in the churchyard of St Mary Magdalene's church with his back to the recumbent granite statue of the saint with her bag of ointment. It is, in many ways, a formal portrait with Causley in smart but casual clothes with a rolled umbrella. Painted by Peter Edwards, it shows the conventional side of Causley with his expression partly hidden by the glint of his large spectacles. There is only a hint of the ironic and humorous nature of the poet. The portrait was hung at the National Portrait Gallery before being shown at the Lawrence House Museum in Launceston. It is now hung in the refurbished Victorian Town Hall in Launceston.

According to Peter Edwards' cousin, a knowledgeable Shropshire man who regularly volunteers at the Lawrence House Museum, the artist left out a whole course of masonry below the recumbent statue so that Causley's head is positioned just below Mary Magdalene's granite drapery. It is a striking painting that demands to be displayed in a large room.

Causley wanted to continue teaching in some capacity so he approached Ronald Tamplin at Exeter University. Tamplin was able to find funds to pay Causley an hourly rate for a weekly seminar at the university and some other work with students as well. Every Tuesday Causley crossed the border on his way to 'Devonshire's' county town and helped organise and lead poetry seminars. Causley's enthusiastic and conscientious work at the university was leading to opportunities for foreign travel in the English speaking world.

Before embarking on journeys Causley had returned to an old passion, the theatre. In 1978 he returned to one of his favourite themes in 'The Gift of a Lamb: A Shepherd's Tale of the first Christmas, told as a verse play.' He looked back to his 1940 Nativity play 'Journey of the Magi' but concentrated on the verse to convey the message rather than

---

45 Desert Island Discs, 1979.

The giant portrait of Causley at Launceston Town Hall, painted by Peter Edwards.

(Courtesy of Emily Whitfield-Wicks.)

dramaturgy. It was a play for children which showed Causley's mastery of verse narrative. Also in 1978 Causley wrote a long verse narrative for children called 'Three Heads made of Gold' which had much in common with his verse dramas. Although neither of these works are set in Cornwall they are told in a Cornish way which would appeal to later Cornish theatre companies such as Kneehigh Theatre.

The most accomplished piece of theatre by Causley is *The Ballad of Aucassin and Nicolette*, written slightly earlier in 1974 but not performed until 1978 by Britain's South West Music Theatre at the Exeter Festival. The play was ambitious in scope and in the number of performers. The story bears more than a passing resemblance to the mediaeval story of Tristan and Yseult and contains the European conventions of courtly love. There is also some down-to-earth bawdy humour from the old Cornish mediaeval dramas and elements harking back to the Cornish *Ordinalia* in the use of simple verse and structured repetition.

The theme of unconventional love which never runs a smooth course is typical of the Middle Ages. Aucassin, the son of a count, falls in love with Nicolette, a Saracen captive. The lovers are separated and eventually reunited after many adventures. There is surreal comedy in the ridiculous war being fought in Torelore where the weapons of mass destruction turn out to be mushrooms, eggs, cheese and rotten apples. In the published version of the play Causley explained his ideas: 'In this present form, the text will be seen to consist of a series of poems and ballads, linked by passages of prose dialogue, and with an absolute minimum of stage direction.' *The Ballad of Aucassin and Nicolette* was broadcast on the BBC in 1980 with David Firth and Imelda Staunton in the title roles. Larger-than-life characters like Martin Oxboy, zany comedy and the search for love all characterise this play as exuberant Causley. The episodic nature of the play can also be seen as deriving from the *Ordinalia* and Cornish mumming and mystery plays.

Through the production of *The Ballad of Aucassin and Nicolette* Causley worked with Stephen McNeff, a composer who asked Causley to write a libretto for the play. This association was to prove beneficial in the coming years.

Surreal comedy also played a part in Causley's next play. *The Doctor and the Devils* was Causley's 1980 adaptation, for the stage, of Dylan Thomas' script. The play is about the Edinburgh body snatchers Burke and Hare, renamed Broom and Fallon. It was Causley's first musical play with musical direction by Stephen McNeff. First performed by Contact

Theatre (Manchester's Young People's Theatre) at the University Theatre in Manchester it was presented in the round, much like the old Cornish mystery plays. It was successful and went on international tour. When Causley was in Banff in western Canada in 1984 he produced the play at the Banff Centre School for Fine Arts.

In 1982 Causley and NcNeff collaborated on a play that has yet to be performed, entitled *The Burning Boy*. Described by Causley as as 'a miracle play for musical theatre' it is based on an episode from the Second Book of Kings in the Bible. In it a Shunammite boy dies of sunstroke in a harvest field, only to be raised from the dead by the prophet Elisha. It can be seen as a modern version of a Cornish mystery play dealing with birth, death and resurrection. To Causley there must have been a certain resonance with the death by fire of his young Victorian aunt in the field near the lime kiln at Trusham. It is a great pity that the play has never been performed; it is not too late for an enterprising theatre company to bring it to the fruition it deserves.

The hiatus of *The Burning Boy* brought Causley back to children's poetry for the middle and late 1980s. However, in 1990, he returned to the theatre, working with Kneehigh Theatre, a Cornish theatre company formed in 1980, on a production of Hans Christian Andersen's *The Tinder Box*. Magical realism characterised this production which, with musical direction by McNeff, went on to tour a number of Cornish schools, including Launceston College. The robust style of production 'with huge, crude props, fantastic costumes, audience involvement, small shocks and surprises from a team of actors well versed in the epic style' proved to be truly Cornish and continued and built on an ancient tradition.

The success of *The Tinder Box* led Causley to adapt Andersen's story *The Emperor's New Clothes* which went on tour in 1990 and 1991. Even more successful was his adaptation of his Cornish poem about a young man and a mermaid, *The Young Man of Cury*, which toured in 1992 and, most popular of all, a 1994 adaptation of his 1970 collection of children's poems *Figgie Hobbin* which toured Cornwall.

Causley's final theatrical work involved McNeff. Based on *The Life and Fables of Aesop* by Sir Roger L'Estrange, written in 1679, it was called *Aesop, A New Opera*, with libretto by Causley. First performed by The National Youth Music Theatre at Blackheath Concert Halls in 1991, it told how Aesop the Ethiopian was enslaved, taken to Greece in the sixth century, became a teller of wise tales and an advisor to politicians and kings and was assassinated by enemies. Causley treats it as a 'classical' musical mystery play with such characters as the hare and the tortoise represented by tourists with a back pack and a camera.

In the opinion of Dr Alan M. Kent, Causley's contribution to Cornish theatre is enormous and has not yet been fully acknowledged. Causley's Cornishness is mainly in his expression and sense of humour rather than in any self-conscious promotion of himself as a Cornish playwright. His drama and his musical collaboration have been overshadowed by the success of his poetry; his writing of plays began before his serious poetry and developed alongside of it, complementing it.

In the Dome Car

In the late 1970s Causley was in his early sixties, retired, healthy and financially secure. He looked and acted younger than his age and was ready to travel further than his usual European destinations. He was delighted to be invited to spend six months as writer-in-residence at the University of Western Australia at Perth and at the Footscray Institute of Technology in Victoria.

Always very much aware that travel comes at a price he prepared for a lengthy time away from home. In his poem 'Night Before a Journey' (*CP*, p.298.) he imagines his house empty with him no longer there. His description of the empty rooms makes us think of the 'little airs' in Virginia Woolf's *To the Lighthouse*, set in Scotland but modelled on places in West Cornwall, that blow round the Ramsey family's empty house fading the wallpaper and making the deserted rooms dusty and forlorn. Causley's old problem was homesickness; a dividing of himself into two disparate halves, the settled, home loving man and the adventurer in foreign parts. There the two entities could only be temporarily joined; a permanent resolution could only result from a total abandonment of all travel or a permanent residence at Cyprus Well. To Causley the latter choice was unthinkable, so he prepared to travel to Australia like a bungee jumper readying himself for a dizzying leap from a viaduct. We must bear in mind the lines of the fourth verse of 'Night before a Journey':

> Nothing in the stopped house
> Shall unbalance the air.
> There is one, says the house-ghost,
> Who is always here.

('Night Before a Journey,' *CP*, p.298 v.4.)

The temporarily united two halves of Causley flew out to Australia to take up his appointments and to be shown the fine cities, pastoral landscapes and red desert heart of the country. He describes the long journey with its numerous flights with stopovers in Bahrain, Damascus and Singapore due to a Qantas Airline strike. Five days after leaving Cornwall he arrived in Melbourne to exclaim: 'Dear Christ, what's this? Myself.' ('Returning South,' *CP*, p.310 v.4.)

Many of Causley's Australian poems were written after his return to Cornwall and included in his collection *Secret Destinations*, published by Macmillan in 1984 and dedicated to Michael Hanke. He visited Australia twice in the late 1970s and early 1980s so his poems are a composite of his travels there. The order in which he presents them in *Secret Destinations* and *Collected Poems 1951 – 2000* are as a journey beginning in Melbourne, proceeding north-east to Sydney, north to the Northern Territories and south-west to the interior and Alice Springs. From there he went south-west to Perth in Western Australia.

Causley used a lot of free verse in his Australian poems, an enormous contrast to much of his work to date, often closing the verse with a Shakespearian rhyming couplet. In 'The Dancers' (*ibid.*, p.315.) he breaks up rhyming couplets to give a sinuous rhythm in line with the aboriginal dancers. He quotes advertisements and billboards in 'Pinchgut' (*ibid.*, p.313.) just as he had years before when referring to his first visit to Sydney in 'HMS Glory at Sydney' (*ibid.*, p.8.). The use of new forms by Causley shows him responding to new stimuli and new challenges. He continued to evolve and experiment as a poet until, in extreme old age, he was no longer able to write.

Being away from home brought back the theme of loss so often present in his poems. Being far from home exposed him to a sadness and a realisation that, apart from his close friends, he was very much alone in the world. He tended to dwell on the harshness of the landscape in the interior and on the destructive force of the ocean. At times his home-sickness overwhelms him with a sense of loss that reminds him of past loves and friends who have gone forever. He constantly noticed the litter, the tin cans, wrecked cars and mining waste always present in the interior. At times he appears to have had enough of Australia, needing to go home in order to place it in perspective.

Half-hidden by drifts of blue rain. Ahead,
The blue rain as we move, the two us, from where
The dryness of jarrah comes to a sudden stop:
You, in another season; I in Manjimup.

('Manjimup,' CP, p.328 v.5.)

It is often very hard to work out Causley's stance in many of his poems because he is seldom didactic. He explores different stances in a truly empathetic way which belies the often straightforward lines on the page. The many meanings of his poems can deliberately vary from reader to reader, much as Causley intended. He presents us with images which he often leaves us to interpret in our own ways. When asked if he had a 'message' he replied that if he had one then it was for the milkman.

It would be very wrong to assume that Causley was always unhappy in Australia. He did return for a third visit and experienced, at times, the same familiar feelings of separation and loneliness. Some of his angst was in retrospect; he enjoyed the experience of new sights and sounds and new words for everyday objects, many of which he used in his Australian poems. He made friends in Australia such as Jeanne and Brian Matthews[46] and was royally entertained and shown the sights.

In 1984 Causley set out once again from home to spend six months in Alberta, in the mountainous west of Canada. He had been asked to work as writer-in-residence at the University of Banff producing plays and taking poetry seminars. Once more he exchanged his familiar 'bright glass cabin' at Cyprus Well for the dome car, the vista dome coach on the Canadian transcontinental railway which took him from Toronto to Banff. Always the keen observer, Causley enjoyed the journey and arrived in Banff ready for the work with students that he so enjoyed.

While in Banff he found out about The Rev. Robert Terrill Rundle, a Cornish Methodist missionary who was employed by the Hudson's Bay Company to work with various tribes of First Nations in the Rupert Land area of northern Saskatchewan. Born in Mylor in West Cornwall, Rundle had little training and suffered from poor health in Canada. Nevertheless he travelled overland all the way west to Alberta and the Rocky Mountains. A mountain near Banff is named after him. Causley identi-

---

46 Professor Brian Matthews FAHA met Causley when teaching English at Exeter University. He went on to become the Head of the Sir Robert Menzies Centre of Australian Studies at the University of London.

fied with his physical unsuitability as a missionary as well as his obvious sensitive nature. His poem 'Under Mount Rundle' (*ibid.*, p.302.) describes Rundle travelling into the mountains to meet the Blackfeet with whom he was to establish a very warm relationship. Rundle and Causley have a lot in common; to paraphrase a quote referring to the late Mrs Ching on a stained glass window of St Mary Magdalene's church in Launceston: 'He hath done what he could.' Both Causley and Rundle sometimes felt that they were unsuited to certain roles and battled against self doubt and a certain amount of depression.

Snow, ice and cold were all anathema to Causley. In his poem 'Bank-head' (*ibid.*, p.300.) Causley describes an abandoned mining town with its familiar, to a Cornishman, array of deserted mining buildings and acres of spoil heaps. He describes an old photograph of the miners who worked there, no doubt with the usual proportion of 'Cousin Jacks' or expatriate Cornish miners, looking vaguely like soldiers from the Great War. Once more Causley's division into two parts is present as he is reminded of home and of a past long gone.

The same themes of dislocation and separation that are present in 'Magpie' (*ibid.*, p.299.), are to be found in the work of many Cornish writers and poets. It would be easy to think that every time Causley travelled he fell briefly in love with one of his companions only to realise all too soon that it would not last. Although quite plausible as a theory, the references to falling out of love occur in well over half of his Australian and Canadian poems. It is more probable that Causley's relationship with the country in which he was staying went through the usual stages of enthusiastic initial acceptance then later rejection followed by a working relationship that no longer involve love or hatred of any aspects of that country.

Once home from his sojourns in Australia and Canada, Causley prepared a new collection of his poems for publication. Entitled *Secret Destinations* his first book of poems entirely for adults for some time was published in hardback by Macmillan in early 1984. It contains an interesting collection of his Australian and Canadian poems as well as a number of autobiographical poems such as 'Seven Houses' (*ibid.*, p.275.); 'The Boot Man' (*ibid.*, p.284.); and 'On Launceston Castle' (*ibid.*, p.286.). One has the impression that he is taking stock of his life since his mother's death and his retirement. There are also some poems about members of his family: 'Richard Bartlett,' 'Dora' and 'Uncle Stan.' Two further poems, 'At the Church of St Anthony, Lisbon' (*ibid.*, p.288.) and 'Greek Orthodox, Melbourne' (*ibid.*, p.319.) show Causley unsympathetic to religion in foreign places. Perhaps this is another manifestation of his dislocation of personality when travelling. Certainly Australia in particular provoked in him old regrets and sad memories of loss which probably harked back to the war.

Secret Destinations did not universally receive the critical acclaim of past collections. Many critics praised his experimentation with different poetic forms and acknowledged his continual development and growth as a major poet. Others expressed slight disappointment in his subject matter. His Australian and Canadian poems might not be among his very best but they repay the attention of numerous readings. One never exactly feels that he is out of his depth but rather that he is not entirely as present in these poems as he is in those set closer to home. He may well wish us to think this; part of him is sharing Cyprus Well with the 'house ghost.'

Another new departure for Causley in *Secret Destinations* is translation. His version of 'Sleeper in a Valley' (*ibid.*, p.295.) is derived from a poem by Jean-Arthur Rimbaud about the futility of war, demonstrated by a handsome youth who appears to be peacefully sleeping in a quiet valley. It is only on seeing the two small holes in his side that we realise that he is dead. The poem has much of the graphic quality of a pre-Raphaelite painting or, closer to home, a painting of the Newlyn School.

There is also a German influence in some of the poems in *Secret Destinations*. Causley had previously spent time in Germany with friends and had met Michael Hanke, who was to become his secretary from 1980 until 1982 when Hanke returned to Germany to take his Ph.D., marry and embark on his teaching career. After a correspondence with Hanke, which began in 1979, Causley invited him to visit him in Cornwall in the Autumn of that year. In 1980 Causley returned to Germany at Hanke's invitation. The two friends spent three weeks travelling from Rendsburg (on the Kiel Canal) south to Frankfurt and the Black Forest visiting friends and relatives of Hanke. To mark his friendship with Hanke Causley later dedicated *Secret Destinations* to him.

For over two years Michael Hanke lived at Cyprus Well. He and Causley became very good friends and worked closely together. Both men enjoyed the friendship and companionship of the other, respecting the boundaries that were important to each of them. Recently Dr Hanke wrote to me:

'While I was with Causley at Cyprus Well from early 1980 until mid-

1982, we were always perfectly frank with one another about our private lives – except that there wasn't much for me to be frank about. One evening he asked me to tell him "everything" about myself. "What is it you want to know specifically?" "Everything," he replied. "That is, if you don't mind." I didn't mind, and so I proceeded to offer what must have been the dullest confession he'd ever heard. He then asked me whether I wanted to know more about him, adding there might be certain facts that might not be to my liking (or words to that effect). After a moment of consideration I said, no. He thanked me and we changed the subject.'

Causley always set himself very high standards of behaviour and morals. It seems to me that his conversation with Hanke could have led to a confession similar to that made by a penitent to a priest. Having heard Hanke's 'confession' he was prepared to reply in kind. We know from his diaries how self-critical Causley could be. Dr Hanke continues:

'I know about nothing about his sexual relationships. I suppose he would have told me if I had been interested. I do know that he would never have been as ruthless in his dealings with women (or men) as were some of his friends (like Ted Hughes). Apart from that, he was a respected teacher in his home town, and everyone I met in Launceston admired him as a poet and a thoroughly upright character. Irregularities of the kind cultivated by the Bohemians of the thirties and forties (George Barker, Dylan Thomas, W. S. Graham) were anathema to him. When I once suggested that he accompany me on a visit to George Barker, he good-naturedly but firmly declined. "A short time with George goes a long way with me."'

Hanke had probably not read Causley's wartime diaries. Had he done so, he would have recognised Causley as a shy but definitely hetero-sexual Cornishman.

Causley had become increasingly open to the influence on him of other countries. There was much that drew him to Germany as well as to the warmer Mediterranean lands. In 'Gudow' (*ibid.*, p.290.) Causley describes the imposition of the iron curtain, the border between West and East Germany, on the world of nature. He had visited Germany with his friend D. M. Thomas and had been struck by the strangeness of the border between West and East. Thomas was impressed by how quickly Causley took in the essence of what he saw without taking notes or spending much time in the vicinity of the border. 'Friedrich' (*ibid.*, p.292.) is a humorous poem about a romantic and feckless young German friend who has constant fantasies about making his fortune.

Another of Causley's translations is 'The Fiddler's Son' (*ibid.*, p.291.), an anonymously written German poem. It is obvious that Causley felt better, more cheerful and more sure of himself, closer to home. Despite his good times in Australia at the end of the war European countries appealed much more to him.

Many of the poems in *Secret Destinations* are poems of regret, an admission of lost youth and lost friendships. In 'Friedrich' there are some very telling lines hidden among humorous observations:

> … His wife Peachey's
> A sorceress. They don't
>
> Say much when I'm around
> But I know they've something
> Going between them better than
> *Collected Poems*, a T.S.B. account
>
> Twelve lines in *Gems*
> *Of Modern Quotations*
> And two (not war) medals.[47]

('Friedrich,' CP, p.292 v.4-6.)

It is typical of Causley that these lines are understated and almost hidden. He is actually talking about young Friedrich and his wife; his observations about his own situation are almost throwaway and not meant to be dwelt on. Here he is at his most ironic but also at his most raw. Surely he doesn't mean us to take him seriously! A momentary regret; but would Causley really have put aside his poetry for a happy marriage?

At the age of sixty-five Causley began to receive his old age pension in robust good health. He was still growing as a poet and was vigorously resisting any form of stereotyping in his work. His old interest in drama and the theatre had resurfaced and he had begun to write plays again. Some of his best poems were still to be written.

---

47 The two medals were (in 1982): The Queen's Gold Medal for Poetry (1967) and The Cholmondely Award for Poetry (1971). Others would follow.

Here We Go Round the Round House

In 1967 Causley had received the Queen's Gold Medal for Poetry and the Cholmondely Award for Poetry in 1971. He ventured up to London in best bib and tucker in 1986 to be made Companion of the British Empire (CBE) at Buckingham Palace. Although he never sought out awards and honours he was happy to receive them when others nomin-ated him for them. His poet friends such as Ted Hughes and Phillip Lar-kin encouraged him to stand for poet laureate when Sir John Betjeman died in 1984.

Many people today firmly believe that Causley should have become poet laureate, either in 1984 or after the death of Ted Hughes in 1998. As a poet Causley was very much his own man. Although deliberately not in the forefront of the innovation of poetic form he would certainly have been up to the job. Temperamentally he would probably not have enjoyed writing poetry to order to commemorate certain royal events. As a young man he had briefly believed that London was the centre of the world but sensibly decided that Launceston and his 'bright glass cabin' would do much better. He was a shy man who did not particularly enjoy public occasions; he very much enjoyed the company of close friends but could sometimes be withdrawn and distant, although never impolite. As an old Launceston friend put it: "Sometimes he could blow hot, blow cold." To function as a poet he needed his own space and he didn't suffer fools gladly. He would have been happy to receive the 'butt of sack' and, with Cornish economy, would have made it last a long time.

He was very happy to receive the award of an honorary doctorate from the University of Exeter in 1977. His close connections with the university and the good work he had done there made the award entirely appropriate. He is one of the few honorary Ph.Ds who was regularly referred to as 'Dr Causley' and can certainly not be seen as a celebrity who was brought in to the university graduation ceremony to say a few words and temporarily enhance the image of the establishment. His reward was apposite and was later to be repeated by the Open University.

During the 1970s and 1980s Causley had had individual poems and short collections published, often in limited editions, by small publishers all over the country. Midnag, in Ashington, Northumberland, a town known for its coal miner artists, published *New Year's Eve, Athens* as a limited edition poetry poster in 1979. Morrigu Press of North Tawton, Devon, brought out a limited edition of *Hymn* in 1983. He was published once again in America; Walker Books in New York produced *Quack! Said the Billy Goat* in 1986.

Causley's interest in drama had never waned. In 1978 Robson published a verse play called 'The Gift of a Lamb.' That same year *The Ballad of Aucassin and Nicolette* came out. It was Causley's most important play to date and contained the blank verse poem 'My Name is Martin Oxboy' (*CP*, p.341.) which Causley used to read in a faux Cockney accent. The character of Oxboy is part sinister part comic and makes us think at times of Caliban. The play was a success and caused Causley to think about his pre-war plays. He eventually determined that they would no longer be produced; he saw them very much as juvenilia. It is a pity that they are not revived; they are short, entertaining and fun. Amateur drama groups would have a lot of fun staging these fast paced plays.

When Causley was in Banff he had adapted Dylan Thomas' unpublished play 'The Doctor and the Devils' to be performed for the first time at the Banff Centre in 1984. With Stephen McIntyre as Billy Bedlam and Ruth Borman as Alice it was accompanied by Causley's broadsheet 'Verses for a First Night' written specially for the performance.

As he continued to develop his poetic voice in the 1980s Causley continued to enjoy his life at Cyprus Well. He enjoyed videos of *Dad's Army* and spaghetti westerns, played the piano in his writing room, read widely and welcomed many of his friends in his house. Ted Hughes often came over from North Devon to visit. Seamus Heaney, called 'Famous Seamus' by his Cornish friend, collaborated with Causley and Hughes for the Arvon Foundation. Local friends such as Arthur Wills came to maintain his clocks and talk. The artist Robert Tilling who had illustrated some of Causley's work, including 'Sleeper in a Valley,' and one of Causley's oldest friends Stanley Simmonds often called in for a talk and a cup of tea.

Causley was fast approaching his seventieth birthday and many of his friends collaborated on the production of a book called simply *Causley at 70*. It was published by Harry Chambers at Peterloo Poets from Calstock, a small town beside the River Tamar a few miles downstream from Launceston. Printed in Plymouth, it was very much a local product, even though it contained contributions from as far afield as America and Australia. Cornish poets and writers played a major part in this book: D. M. Thomas, J. C. Trewin, and Bill Manhire wrote tributes in prose and poetry to their friend in 'Lanson.'

Among the most perceptive tributes was the short essay 'Faithful Travelling' by D. M. Thomas, an old friend and travelling companion from West Cornwall. Thomas praised his friend's quiet but deep observation of a border post at Gudow on the frontier between West and East Germany:

'From his description I remembered it all, yet why hadn't I noticed it at the time? 'My God!' I thought. 'Why didn't *I* see it?' The three of us had stood quietly for a few minutes, observing, reflecting; Charles had not whipped-out a notebook and biro, nor clicked a camera; yet it seemed, on my reading of his poem, as if his eye or his mind were fitted with some ultra-sensitive technology, which enabled him to read unerringly; at the same time to find the simple unerring metaphor.' (*Causley at 70*, p.10.)

Thomas' perceptive tribute at the end of his short piece is one of the most sincere and memorable of the whole book:

'I was once introducing him [Causley] to a student-group at an Arvon Course in Devon, and for the first and only time in my life I completely dried. I became literally dumb. What was in my mind was the huge distance he had travelled from the struggling working-class home in Launceston, between the wars. His vision encompassed the world, and the world of art; yet he had remained faithful to his origins, his voice still held the tones of moorland granite, the sea, and soft Tamar-side valleys. I glimpsed the effort, the courage, behind all his faithful travelling. Who could tell that from his laconic, friendly manner, that humorous, throwaway Cornish speech? The thought moved me deeply – and that's why I lost my tongue.' (*ibid.*, p.11)

Other tributes were less personal: there was an assessment of his work by the American academic Dana Gioia (*ibid.*, p.28) whom he had met on a reading tour at Hastings-on-Hudson, New York in 1984. Fay Zwicky wrote a piece of Australian blank verse, 'The Call' (*ibid.*, p.18) from a solar phone box at William Creek, South Australia.

Ted Hughes, with his usual incisive perception, wrote a poem to Causley entitled 'Birthday Greetings' which ends with the lines:

Congratulations, Charles.
God gave us half the wit
To recognise our own
And to stick with it.

(ibid., p.13.)

Philip Larkin wrote a witty and appropriately laconic poem 'A Birthday Card' which began with these lines:

Dear CHARLES, my muse, asleep or dead,
Offers this doggerel instead
To carry from the frozen North
Warm greetings for the twenty-fourth ...

(ibid., p.39)

Anthony Thwaite supplied a short parody of Causley's poetry resurrected from 1972 (*ibid.*, p.71) and Seamus Heaney sent a few translated lines from *Beowulf* (*ibid.*, p.70) on the role of the poet.

Some of the most remarkable material came from Causley himself. 'Timothy Winters' was reprinted with an ink-spotted drawing of the boy with suitably ragged hair and fingers in close proximity to grimy nostrils, drawn by Ralph Steadman (*ibid.*, p.73). Other poems, written and chosen by Causley, were included in the book. Two new poems were included; 'In 1933' (*ibid.*, p.75) looks backwards to a Guy Fawkes firework display on Castle Green in Launceston and 'Eden Rock' (*ibid.*, p.74) looks both backwards and forward to the completion of the circle of birth and death.

Other remarkable contributions by Causley are the drafts in his handwriting of 'Immunity' (*ibid.*, p.80) with all the overwriting, corrections and alterations. Two rare autobiographical pieces of prose 'A Kitchen in the Morning' (*ibid.*, p.94) and 'So Slowly to Harbour' (*ibid.*, p.106) give us insights into Causley's early years and the slow five-year decline of his mother towards her death.

In *Causley at 70* Causley 'gives as good as he gets'; not content with sitting back to praise and adulation he gives the reader a rare insight into the struggles and joys of different periods of his life. He fills in some of the gaps and supplies us with much local colour both in his prose pieces and his poems such as 'Bridie Wiles' (*ibid.*, p.77). His keen observation and sense of humour undimmed he prepared to face the long years of his old age.

Ted Hughes' premature death from cancer in 1998 robbed Causley of one of his dearest and most faithful friends. For the best part of thirty-five years Causley and Hughes had been close. Causley had known Sylvia Plath, Hughes' first wife, and had been devastated by her suicide in the early sixties. Indeed she had shown him their infant children in their cots when they first moved to Devon. He was now faced with the problem of who would be poet laureate for a second time.

He was obviously capable of becoming an excellent poet laureate. Once again he refused to chase the honour and was quite happy when Andrew Motion, a much younger poet and an eminent encourager of other poets, was awarded the laureate. In the event Motion only agreed to keep it for ten years and found the post inhibiting as a poet. So many of Causley's fellow poets had died: Louis MacNeice, Siegfried Sassoon, W. H. Auden, W. H. Graham, Philip Larkin and Ted Hughes had all gone. Causley though had many local friends with whom he shared his life and enthusiasms.

Father Anthony Maggs was a Roman Catholic priest who belonged to the Order of Augustinian Canons, who were based at St Thomas' Priory in Launceston before Henry VIII greedily dissolved and ruined the monastery. In 1881 the Augustinians had returned to Cornwall and took charge of the Catholic church in Launceston on the hill leading to St Stephens. Father Maggs was priest in various Cornish churches and became a firm friend of Causley. He and Causley first met at an ecumenical Harvest Festival service in the moorland church at St Clether in the early 1970s. They became friends and Causley showed Father Maggs places in Cornwall he had never seen. Over the years the two men would drive to a place of historic interest, often a church, share the cost of a pub lunch and talk about all sorts of subjects including the progress of Causley's current poems.

Causley was fascinated by the history of St Cuthbert Mayne, the Roman Catholic priest hanged, drawn and quartered in the square in Launceston in 1588. A more modern priest also fascinated him; Father Bernard Walke was a socialist 'high church' Anglican priest from the New Forest who became the parish priest at St Hilary, inland from

Marazion in West Cornwall 'between two Cornish seas.' Walke was a pacifist and a friend of George Bernard Shaw, who praised Walke's nativity plays that were broadcast annually by the BBC from 1924 until 1936. He was also an artist and a writer; his book *Twenty Years at St Hilary* has become a Cornish classic. Walke had an enormous effect on Causley. He became a key influence and an example of a Christian who achieved much through his ideas and example.

When Causley and Father Maggs finally visited St Hilary after the long drive from Launceston the result was, as so often happened, a poem, 'At St Hilary' (*CP*, p.357.) A copy of the poem, handwritten by Causley, came later to Father Maggs in *Twenty-One Poems*.[48] The little church at St Hilary had been mainly rebuilt after a fire in Victorian times and vandalised by an iconoclastic 'low church' Kensitite[49] mob in 1932.

Causley had a lot in common with Father Walke: pacifism, nativity plays and dedicated service to the public. The question of Causley's attitude to the Christian faith remains; his poem 'At St Hilary' gives us perhaps his final answer.

Through rain and wind and risen snow
I come, as fifty years ago,

Drawn by I know not what, to sound
A fabled shore, unlost, unfound,

Where in the shadow of the sun
Past, present, future, wait as one.

('At St Hilary,' *CP*, p.357 vv.6-8.)

Causley's 'fabled shore, unlost, unfound' is, in my opinion, the God who exists quite independently of man and has to be sought out by the individual. There are many ways of doing this and many ways of failing. All through his long life Causley was acutely aware of the failings of mankind and especially of his own failings. Here we have God as an

---

48 *Twenty One Poems* was published in a limited edition by Celandine Press in Shipton-on-Stour, Warwickshire in 1986.

49 Kensitites were fanatical followers of John Kensit, 1853 – 1902, who founded The Protestant Truth Society to oppose the Anglican 'High Church' Oxford Movement. On August 8th 1932 a fifty-strong Kensitite mob locked Father Walke out of his church at St Hilary and destroyed many of the 'idolatrous' church fittings, most of which were cheap substitutes provided by Walke when he heard that they were coming.

objective reality who has always existed, 'fabled' because of mankind's various recorded attempts to find Him. There is a marked parallel in Causley's theology between the passage of time with its inevitable end and the Holy Trinity 'that was and is and will be' in the line 'Past, present, future, wait as one'.[50]

It was inevitable that as Causley grew old his thoughts turned to the survival of the soul. Having the example and friendship of devout Christians past and present must have helped to answer some of the important questions that preoccupied him.

Cream teas at Crackington Haven with friends old and new and men like Stanley Simmonds and Father Anthony Maggs made his life a great pleasure. He was not a man to just drop in on, arrangements had to be made in advance and pleasurable visits planned and happily anticipated. Causley had to be ready to receive visitors; he had to put away the inward looking part of himself and bring out the more extrovert side. Friends were remembered when Causley travelled; postcards arrived from him from 'all four corners of the imagined earth' with warm and witty messages for his friends.

As time passed Causley gave up his car. Never a confident nor an enthusiastic driver, he did not sell the vehicle but gave it away to the son of a neighbour. He was happy to be driven around provided that he paid his share of the petrol and the pub lunches and cream teas. He would often just sit in a church, his mind working beneath the placid exterior of his well dressed self. He did take notes but often memorised lines of the poems he composed before writing them down in longhand and altering them with a merciless scrutiny.

Pinky and Kensey, the beloved cats of Cyprus Well, had become old and infirm and had finally died. Rupert, a magnificent ginger cat who had been brought down from Scotland to live with the neighbours Mr and Mrs Wright, was displaced by the acquisition of a large dog and soon adopted Causley. An amicable arrangement with the neighbours legalised the adoption and Rupert 'came over the wall' and moved into Cyprus Well to become Causley's constant companion.

After the publication of *Twenty-One Poems* in 1986 Causley continued

---

50 Shades of T. S. Eliot's 'Four Quartets': 'In my beginning is my end.' (Four Quartets, East Coker) and:
　　　'Time present and time past
　　　Are both perhaps present in time future
　　　And time future contained in time past.'
　　(Four Quartets, Burnt Norton.)

to write adventurously. Dr Dana Gioia wrote:

'Rather than retreating into one familiar style or set of subjects, Causley pursues a fascinating dialectic – both thematically and technically. Balancing the inner and outer worlds, he writes alternatively of the past and present, the personal and the public, deliberately shifting his tone between the subjective and objective, while composing in both free verse and formal verse.' (*Causley at 70*, p.34-35.)

Although Gioia wrote this for Causley's seventieth birthday it remains true to the end of his life. The quantity of his poems diminished but not the quality or originality. Causley seldom descended into repetition or sentimentality; nostalgia and a certain wistfulness played their part. The passing of time was not always seen as the enemy, it revealed memories previously imprisoned. The loss of memory was far worse. Among Causley's most interesting late poems are those about his family: crazy aunts and uncles who lived and died both in Cornwall and 'Devonshire.'

In 1990 Causley was honoured with the award of the Ingersoll/T. S. Eliot Prize for Poetry, a high award that confirmed his place as one of the few leading poets of the twentieth century.

As Causley became an old man his youthful demeanour began to fade. His eyes became somewhat veiled by their heavy lids and pronounced bags underneath. He retained a full head of somewhat unruly grey hair and the lines at the corners of his eyes showed that he had lost none of his sense of humour. He was a handsome old man who was becoming somewhat frail in his old age. His walks up the steep hill into town took longer and demanded more pauses. He was seldom lonely in his secret house at Cyprus Well, children would often come to visit him and were always welcome. Adult friends often came round and took him out. His life continued to be pleasantly independent. It was shared by his similarly purring ginger feline companion.

One of his last trips abroad was to a lovely hilltop Italian village where Causley sat in the sun. He even made friends with a black and white cat who he photographed several times. The last photo in the series shows the cat sleeping peacefully on Causley's lap.

He now wrote poetry at a more leisurely pace, often returning to classical poetic forms. As he told John Walsh in November 1998:

'It's a good discipline not to go sprawling on. People remember you better that way. And a poem has to match its subject. But really, the whole thing is just as much a mystery to me now as when I started.'

In the same article Walsh sums up the essence of the subject matter of Causley's poetry:

'Causley's subject has always been innocence: the fragility of innocence: the rupture and brutalising of and loss and death of innocence. In his poems, childhood's end, the betrayal of love, the rejection of God and the onset of cynicism are all part of the same sad, entropic tendency.'

Even so, much of the poetry is suffused with a humour which can be dark but is, in essence, very Cornish. Causley knew what worked for him and was determined never to force his ideas on his reading public. Never once did he insult the reader's intelligence.

He continued to enjoy his readings and broadcasts. When in London to read his poems he often noticed the actor and *Crackerjack* presenter Leslie Crowther in the audience. He was always pleased to see him; Crowther, with his impeccable sense of timing, always clapped and laughed in exactly the right places.

Causley was still a regular fixture around the town of Launceston in his blue Breton cap and mackintosh to protect him against the frequent drizzle. The cap suited him; it marked him out as a Celt and as a sailor.

After the publication of *Early in the Morning* in 1986 and *Jack the Treacle Eater* in 1987 Causley continued to write collections of poems for children. During the 1990s four books of children's poems were published: *The Young Man of Cury and Other Poems* (1991); *All Day Saturday* (1994); *Collected Poems for Children* (1996); and *The Merrymaid of Zennor* (1999). These collections were popular and well received but did not always have the impact that *Figgie Hobbin* had back in 1970. Causley was not declining as a poet as his few adult poems from his old age also show. He never lost the ability to surprise his readers.

Causley's accountant Les Baker became a close friend. Les took care of Causley's taxes and looked after his growing savings. His wife Margaret also became a favourite. At a supper in Launceston Causley cheekily looked at the food on her husband's plate, noticing that he had taken a little more than he had. Turning to Les he said: "You must have insides like Hoskins' boiler!" Les knew when his leg was being pulled; among old friends Causley could get away with a lot. Hoskins was a well-known plumbing and engineering firm in Launceston, situated not far from the Town Hall in Western Road.

The Bakers lived in the old St Thomas' vicarage up the steep St Catherine's hill from the semi-industrial area where Causley had been

Charles Causley at the book signing at the Eagle House Hotel in Launceston.

(Copyright Sean Hernon.)

born. They named their house Victoria House from a former home and often entertained Causley to tea in the afternoon. They were Launceston born and bred and thoroughly understood their town and its people.

June Wills faithfully cleaned Causley's house on a regular basis and enjoyed his company. She took over from Mrs Stanmore while Mark drove Causley to appointments in his taxi and did errands for him.

Causley's eightieth birthday was celebrated with great joy by all his many friends. He was the doyen of poets and was visited and interviewed by Dr Dana Gioia, who noticed that he was easily moved to tears. Causley knew his own worth and place as a poet, insisting to Gioia that he was not just a local poet but a poet in the wider world who based many of his poems in Launceston and Cornwall. He was never a competitive man and never suffered jealousy at the achievements of others. Having worked out his place in the world Causley was content to live out his life where he was most happy, in the town where he grew up and had his career.

To mark Causley's eightieth birthday Launceston Civic Society put a small square stone monument beside St Thomas Water, near his birthplace. Causley would have appreciated the unconscious irony of its placing; it is found just across the road from the entrance to St Thomas' churchyard. It is nearer to Causley's mother's grave and to his future grave than to his birthplace. The flag of St Piran was flown from the castle top to mark Causley's birthday. This tradition continues during the days of the Charles Causley Festival every year in early June.

In the year 2000 the final, and definitive, collection of his poetry was published in his lifetime. Published by Picador, an imprint of Pan Macmillan, it was entitled *Charles Causley: Collected Poems 1951 – 2000 Revised Edition*. As usual the poems and their order were selected by Causley. The collection begins with 'Keats at Teignmouth, Spring 1818' and ends with 'Eden Rock.' The enigmatic figure surveying the snowy landscape on the cover seems more suitable to Yorkshire than Cornwall. The walls channelling the figure are too thin to be granite. Shades of Ted Hughes.

Neil Burden and his wife, who lived at Trecarrel Manor, would take Causley out on trips to local places of interest, including Trago Mills, a huge and quirky shopping centre between Liskeard and Bodmin. Causley also celebrated several Christmases and birthdays at Trecarrel.

His contented life at Cyprus Well could not last forever. His red United Kingdom passport would expire in 2002 but Causley had no real desire to travel. It is interesting to see inside the passport that the next of kin to contact in emergencies was 'Mrs Cynthia Simmonds.' In 2001, the first true year of the new century, after suffering a few small strokes, Causley suffered a heavy fall in his house and had to be taken to the local twenty bed hospital in Launceston. While in hospital he began to make a good recovery and joked with the nurses: "Take care of me. I'm a national treasure." He retained his robust sense of irony and humour in his hospital bed. At the age of eighty-four he knew that his life would change and that, for him, independent living was at an end.

He chose to move to to Kernow House Nursing Home on the southern edge of Launceston for recuperation and never came home again on a permanent basis. He was too old and too frail ever to live alone again, even with the help of his friends and devoted employees. He liked his room at Kernow House. It had a view of the entrance and out to a very busy bird table at the front of the building.

Rupert 'went over the wall' again and was adopted by the Bakers at Victoria House. He was taken once to visit Causley at Kernow House and settled to a life of rural contentment. When Les Baker announced to Causley that he had a visitor the old man replied: "Has it got four legs?" and was delighted to see his old friend. Like his master he lived to a ripe old age. He died in 2007 and was buried beneath a commemorative stone in the Baker's garden which is engraved 'a fine Scottish cat and friend of Charles Causley.'

In 2000 Causley was awarded the Heywood Hill Prize for a Lifetime's Contribution to Literature, a prestigious prize that was worth £15,000. His friend of many years the writer Susan Hill travelled from her home in Gloucestershire to receive the prize for him. Later in the year she received the honour in Causley's name when he was made a Companion of Literature by the Royal Society of Literature. Causley's reply to the assembled Society was: 'My goodness, what an encouragement.'

Friends called on him on a regular basis. Richard Graham, a former hotelier and chef, who had bought the Launceston Bookshop[51] opposite the church porch of St Mary Magdalene's church, came to see him once a week invariably bringing him small packets of inventive surprises.

One such pleasant surprise was an application form for admittance to the 'Just William Fan Club.' Causley had long been a fan of Richmal

---

51 Richard Graham retired from the Launceston Bookshop in August 2012 to begin a well-earned semi retirement.

Crompton's[52] scruffy wartime vagabond and had, in his house at Cyprus Well, a complete set of first editions of the 'Just William' books. When Causley received a letter back from the fan club saying there were no vacancies Graham, Causley and a few friends got together in Causley's room and drafted a set of rules for admission to the rival 'William Brown's Gang' whose headquarters was to be Kernow House. It went as follows:

> Information for members of 'William Brown's Gang'
> In line with current rules and regulations and to comply with all relevant laws the following guidelines have been created.
> 1. There is no longer any strict dress code, all comfortable clothing is allowed, short trousers with braces and caps are no longer obligatory.
> 2. It is advised that you do not argue with any adults or girls, just hear them out, agree with what they say, then ignore them and do what you want to.
> 3. Always use the disposable gloves as they make it unlikely that you will get caught with dirty fingers.
> 4. At all times avoid any girls called Violet Elizabeth who lisp.
> 5. Should you be caught by an adult doing something they think is wrong blame Mr Tony Blair. As adults seem to think he causes most of their problems!
> 6. Always remember that life should be enjoyed so if you don't like it don't do it.[53]

Causley had always had the ability to be childlike without becoming childish. In his extreme old age he retained his ability to laugh and accept his situation. One day someone from the Monkey Sanctuary in Looe came to visit the old people at Kernow House. Causley remarked in a letter to Susan Hill: 'I never thought I'd end up with a blessed monkey in my arms.' He was warm, well fed and comfortable. He could afford to pay for his care at Kernow House without being forced to sell his house at Cyprus Well. It gave him great satisfaction to think of his home with his precious contents continuing under the watchful eyes of his many

---

52 Richmal Crompton, 1890 – 1969, was a suffragette and teacher who turned to writing after contracting polio in her twenties. Her *Just William* books were mainly published during the Second World War.
53 Supplied by Richard Graham.

friends, with the eventual possibility of it becoming a centre for future writers under the aegis of the future Causley Trust.

Causley's old friend Arthur Wills, now a former mayor and a bard of the Gorsedd Kernow, came regularly to visit him. The two friends talked about old times and about people they had both known. They put the world to rights on a regular basis. When talking about politicians Causley would say: "Oh well, they think they're doing a grand job," and "That's alright, but we know don't we."

He knew no self pity; any memories that upset him were of friends who had died during the war or since. His main regret was that he had never married and had children of his own. From time to time Les Baker brought Rupert to Kernow House to visit. The elderly cat took the visits in his stride and then settled down on a chair by the window, where he was photographed fast asleep.

On December 5th 2002 Causley was taken to Victoria House, the home of Les and Margaret Baker, for a recording session of his reading some of his poems. He thoroughly enjoyed the experience; his voice was as firm and as clear as ever. The only problem was Rupert; his sonorous purring while sitting on Causley's lap drowned out his reading when it was played back. The whole session had to be repeated, much to Causley's amusement. The result was a fine recording, fifty minutes of Causley reading some of his favourite poems in a steady voice with pithy comments and a commentary on the 'awful' folly of war. This was the last time he would ever do a reading and he ended it with 'Eden Rock.'

As 2002 merged into 2003 Causley's frail body was wearing out after a series of small strokes and the onset of Parkinson's disease. His mind was as sharp as ever as spring came to North Cornwall.

O spring has set off her green fuses
   Down by the Tamar today,
And careless, like tide-marks, the hedges
   Are bursting with almond and may.

('The Seasons in North Cornwall,' *CP*, p.31 v.1.)

It was to be his last spring; his body declined all through the summer of that year. He celebrated his eighty-sixth birthday on 24th August 2003.

On Tuesday November 4th 2003 the largest solar flare to date was recorded. Charles Stanley Causley, the poet who wrote 'I am the Great

Sun' (*CP*, p.57.), died on that same day in the presence of one of his many friends.

Although his death had been long expected his friends were stunned by the news. How could they envisage Launceston without him? The huge hollow had to be filled; a fitting memorial service in St Mary Magdalene's church was planned. It was to be a service of thanksgiving for his life and took place on Monday December 1st 2003 at 2.30pm, a few days after his funeral at St Thomas' church and burial in the churchyard.

The order of service was plain with a Celtic cross below Causley's full name and dates. On the back page were these lines:

'He has achieved success who has lived well, laughed often and loved much; who has gained the respect of intelligent men and the love of children; who has filled his niche and accomplished his task; who has left the world better than he found it, whether by the perfect poem, or appreciation of the world's beauty and never failing to express it; who has always looked for the best in others, and given the best he had; whose life was an inspiration, whose memory is a benediction.' ANON.

The poems read at the service were: 'By St Thomas Water' (*CP*, p.123.), 'Timothy Winters,' 'Song of the Dying Gunner AA1' and 'Sibard's Well.' Later in the service 'Scenes from Childhood II Paradise' (*ibid.*, p.397.) and 'Fleeing the City' (*ibid.*, p.407.) were also read. Finally 'They're fetching in Ivy and Holly' was read and Richard Baker, son of Les and Margaret Baker and a former pupil of Causley's, read 'Eden Rock.' Other readers included Father Maggs, Hannah Read, a friend and colleague from the National School, and Paul Tyler MP, now Lord Tyler of Goss Moor.

The few hymns sung were simple old favourites often chosen by Causley to be sung at Primary School assemblies.

After the service, in the ecumenical spirit that Causley would have approved of:

' … you are invited to the Central Methodist Hall (just across the road) to partake of a favourite of Charles' – A Cornish Cream Tea.'

Standing at the back of the packed church for the service was the Dartmouth poet Kevin Pyne who recorded his heartfelt impressions in his poem 'At the Memorial Service for Charles Causley.'[54]

Causley had been laid to rest beside his mother in a grave beside the level path across the churchyard of St Thomas' church, a pebble's throw from St Thomas Water and the square stone marking his eightieth birth-

---

54 Reproduced in full below as Appendix 2.

day. His gravestone is simple; on it is inscribed his name, the dates of his birth and death and the plain word 'poet.' The only embellishment apart from the flowing script used on the stone is a finely carved pen and hand. The hand is Causley's own, based on a detail from a photograph of him writing in his study.

His grave is one hundred and eighty-seven paces from the front door of the house in which he was born. Thus was the circle of his earthly life completed.

How It Belongs To Be

Causley left a great deal of money, over a quarter of a million pounds, to be divided between St Thomas' church in Launceston and St Michael's in Trusham. He also left the Trusham house to Stephen McNeff and his wife and two paintings to Father Maggs, one to sell in order to raise money for a memorial window to Father Bernard Walke in St Saviour's church in Polruan, across the river from Fowey. There were also a number of smaller bequests to friends and carers. He left the ownership of the copyright of his poems to Michael Hanke to be administered by Bruce Hunter of David Higham Associates in London. His own affairs he left in the hands of two trustees, Arthur Wills and Les Baker, who he could trust to never let him down.

His house at Cyprus Well was bought by the Causley Trust to be restored as a study centre and temporary home for writers in residence. Repairs have been done and all important papers, letters, diaries and photographs sent off to the Special Collections Library at the University of Exeter by Arthur Wills via Jessica Gardener, where I was able to read them under ideal conditions. To visit the house is a privilege; it is much as it was when Causley lived there in his old age. His bed is made up with a warm feather eiderdown, his blue jacket and tie hang neatly on the wardrobe door. A few of his walking sticks still stand in the little lobby inside the front door. Although his extensive bookshelves are empty most of his eclectic collection of paintings hangs on the fading walls: a portrait of Lord Nelson, a scene from the Holy Land, an old Cornish church.

After twelve years of planning and perseverance the future of Causley's house is secure. Cornwall Council, Arts Council England, Launceston Town Council and the Charles Causley Trust are funding the refurbishment and conservation of 2 Cyprus Well as a writers' retreat or as a base for a writer in residence. The downstairs rooms, the entrance room and study will be conserved as they were when Causley lived there while the bedrooms will be modernised and upgraded, a central heating system installed, the roof reslated and insulated, and the bulging walls tied in. The rear extension has been rebuilt and the kitchen, bathroom and passage remodelled.

Lawrence House Museum has his desk and an excellent exhibition of objects and papers from his long life. Both the Causley Trust and the Causley Society keep his memory alive with walks, meetings and birthday and Christmas services at St Thomas' church. The recently formed Causley Festival in Launceston is going from strength to strength with poets and artists of international status contributing to the programme.

How will Causley's poetic and dramatic legacy stand the test of time? The twenty-first century readers, scholars and academics took time to draw a deep sad breath after Causley's death. War has not gone away, merely fragmented into dusty lands; Causley's observations of human frailty, inconsistency and betrayal will always be proved accurate. His poetic voice will spread as time goes by. In 2012 Michael Hanke edited a collection of critical essays on aspects of Causley's work entitled *Through the Granite Kingdom*.[55] It is readable and perceptive and shows that academia are taking Causley seriously. A new collection of Causley's unpublished poems is being worked on and his later plays will be revived by theatre groups, mainly in Cornwall. Other biographies and memoirs will undoubtedly follow this one. For National Poetry Day 2012 Causley's poem 'I am the Song' (*CP*, p.420.) was chosen as the one poem to be projected onto the wall in Piccadilly Circus, normally advertising National Panasonic and Coca Cola.

Jim Causley, a brilliant young folk singer from East Devon, is descended from Charles Causley's great grandfather, Samuel Causley of Trusham. His parents come from just a stone's throw from Trusham. Jim shares his distant relative's sense of humour and poetic and musical talent. He has set some of Causley's poems to music in such a way as to do them justice. He recorded some of them with a group of like-minded musicians in Cyprus Well using Causley's own piano for the accompaniment.

As the tenth anniversary of Causley's death approaches the number of scholars considering embarking on Ph.Ds and M.A.s in Causley's poetry and drama increases. There will be a new interest in Causley as he

55 Michael Hanke (ed), *Through the Granite Kingdom*, published by Wissenschaftlicher Verlag Trier in 2012.

is seen to emerge from among his twentieth century contemporaries as the truest and most universal poet to come from Cornwall or any other place in the British Isles. He is now seen as much more than the poet of Launceston and North Cornwall. His natural modesty and lack of interest in celebrity can no longer work against him from the grave. In a matter of time he will be seen as one of the greatest British poets of the latter half of the twentieth century.

Men like Dr Alan M. Kent, a Cornish writer, poet, dramatist, academic and teacher are determined to raise Causley's profile. Dr Kent has recently published *The Theatre Works of Charles Causley* which includes several previously unpublished plays.

Dr Malcolm Wright, Chairman of the Charles Causley Society, has written an excellent short biography of Causley entitled *Charles Causley: A Universal Poet* which contains a number of previously unpublished photographs.

On a personal note I know how the memory of 'Charles' is valued in his home town. A few weeks ago, on a wet and blustery day, I drove the fifty miles to Launceston to do some research. I enjoyed a pasty under the dripping lime trees on the old parade ground behind St Mary Magdalene's church and looked over the valley of the Tamar beyond the roof of the house at Cyprus Well to the distant sunlit hills and tors of Dartmoor which looked to me, for all the world, like the Highlands of Scotland. Somewhere up there, I thought, is Eden Rock. Then I walked down steep Ridgegrove Hill past Cyprus Well down into the valley of the Kensey. At the bottom of the hill I paused to look at a small butter well in the hedge and the distant view of steep and isolated Brent Tor over in 'Devonshire.'

An old countryman walking along the lane told me what the well was and said that he had lived in the valley for fifty years. When I asked him if he had known Mr Causley his face lit up.

"Yes," he said. "I remember Charles. Good as gold he was. Taught both of my sons and always had a good word to say. A wonderful man he was, God bless him."

Appendix 1: An Unpublished Poem

Charles Causley's unpublished poem, written in Gibraltar, from his diary 17th October 1940.

'The Swimmers'

(To R)

You who were young with me will know the pool,
The permanent spider in the crumbled wall,
New clipped the urgent ivy, known the cool
Flash of a diver and the wild bird's call,
Touched the bright pattern children and sunshine made
As old September, all her treasures fled
Flung leaf and wind and flame – turned the bright blade
Of grass to rust and trees gave up their dead.
But not for me my pool. Now I am taught
The iron art of war. Yet from its bond
Down the sweet shallows of remembered thought
And the discovered depths that lie beyond
Nightly I swim the waters once again,
Green hung and needled by a country rain.

(first published in *An Baner Kernewek/The Cornish Banner* in 2012)

This early sonnet is very much in the 'home thoughts from abroad' tradition. It is very competent but lacks the brilliance of much of Causley's later work. There is an influence of A. E. Housman, particularly in the lines 'Down the sweet shadows of remembered thought' and an unusually tight *abab* rhyming scheme. In the phrases 'the iron art of war' and 'old September' we see the sure touch of the later poems. The yearning to be back in Launceston reminds us of Causley's Australian poems. The 'R' to whom the poem is dedicated was Russell Uren, the left wing pacifist friend of Causley's from Launceston who served in the Navy in a dangerous non-combatant role and survived the war.

Appendix 2: At the Memorial Service for Charles Causley by Kevin Pyne

They gather here today
The people of the black and gold
One and all so softly spoken
To lend their love to a man
Who never wrote a love poem
Save to his mother
Save to twenty thousand children
Save to a sea of never forgotten souls
And to the places he loved
Which like his life ran
To seaward from the river ford
From where he watched them in silence
Those who walked across his life
Taught them letters and wrote of them
Touching so many
That in the cold church anointed by the
Biting Cornish rain which blew in
From the great winter grey Atlantic
Held at bay by Cornish granite
And coloured glass saints
We stood and sang
Strangers drawn in, yet at home
Made welcome to the church named for a woman
Who had washed the feet of Jesus
To pray and take tea,
In an assembly of those
More at home in a great poet's parlour

Where they felt such a comfort
Called him Charles
As they read his soft saved chosen words
In their soft western voices
Pronounced from beyond the page
Brought to life the words
And smiled to themselves
When they recognised and remembered
Until they were done
And we filed outside
Past the black and white bookshop
In which his words will live
As long as Cornwall
To take tea and scones
In the clean church hall from church hall cups
That chinked as our spoons stirred in
Our first warm words to strangers
Spoken in hushed reverence
In our overcoats and oilskins,
A western Sunday tea
On a wet Cornish Monday.

(*Further up the River, and Fifty Other Poems* by Kevin Pyne, reproduced with the kind permission of Richard Webb, Publisher, Dartmouth, South Devon.)

Appendix 3: An Afternoon With Charles Causley

"Nice to see you; please come in. Mind the step down from the angle of the road. Welcome to Cyprus Well. Good of you to come all this way to see me. From over the Tamar in Devonshire did you say? Exeter, was it? My father was a Trusham man so I know the area quite well.

Come into the living room. A snug little room with a view fore and aft. I see you're looking at the painting of Nelson on the wall; a great man Nelson. You'll meet him in some of the other rooms in the house. He reminds me to keep going, to never give up.

Don't take your shoes off. The carpet is a little worn like its owner. It's a good forty years old, bought by my mother at the Co-op. Please sit down and make yourself comfortable.

Please would you make sure the door is closed to keep Rupert in. He has about three lives left and no doubt will see me out. He adopted me from next door when they brought in a new dog. My mother and I always had a cat and I like to carry on the tradition. Cats and children turn out to be the best judges of character, you see.

From the University are you? I never had the chance to do that, only Teacher Training College in Peterborough. And all those years at sea … Mind you I taught part-time at Exeter University and went over to Canada and Australia, like all good Cornishmen, to work as poet in residence. I loved some of those places as well as some of the ports I visited in the Navy.

Sometimes I think of this room as a cabin, especially in the winter when the wind roars about the town and the rain comes down in sheets. You can hear the water gurgle past in the gutter on its way to the Tamar. But put on the light and shut the curtains and you can feel as snug as a lord in here.

You seem surprised that I have a television and a video player. What are some of my favourites? I love films with Clint Eastwood, particularly the westerns. I also am fond of Dad's Army. I record the programmes from the television and watch them in the evenings when there is noth-ing on.

Yes, I do have some interesting pictures up there by the ceiling. Many are religious but not just in a Christian way. That candlestick on the mantelpiece is a Jewish menorah with room for seven candles.

I see you're looking at the little figure of the dancing bear. My mother gave that to me when I was quite small when we lived on the other side of town by the River Kensey, St Thomas Water. I was born in that house near the river. After my father died we moved because my mother was deathly afraid of the water rats. I still miss being so near to St Thomas' church; I expect I will be buried in the churchyard there one day.

Would you like to see my study? It's just through this door at the bottom of the stairs. Don't fall over the jar that I use as a door stop when I want to go through to the kitchen and the bathroom. It has 'T. CHING, LAUNCESTON' on it and reminds me of young Thomas Ching who went to sea in the reign of King William IV only to be wrecked off the Great Barrier Reef. He was rescued from a raft by canni-bals and is still known in Lanson as 'Eton, Eaton, Eaten Ching.' You can see his monument in St Mary Magdalene's church.

Over there is my desk. When I write I sometimes use the typewriter and sometimes a pen. I haven't bought a computer because I'm quite happy with my typewriter and the library here in town. I keep most of my books in here on these shelves opposite the door. Oh, and there's Nelson again over by the door to remind me of my duty.

I love the view through the window past the kitchen. On the other side of the bottlebrush bush is the little yard where I like to sit out in the summer. It's private and I can take my cup of tea out there in the sun. Down the steps from the yard is my scrap of garden, now rather shaded by that huge cypress tree. You can see my garden shed from here. I won't show it to you because it is not as tidy as it should be!

The sailor's hat over by the window was mine before I became a Petty Officer. Somehow I forgot to hand it back in. I'm sure the pusser didn't miss it. The German *Pickelhaube* from the Great War was brought back from France by my father after he was gassed. If you look inside you can see the name 'TED' written in pencil. The war did for my father. He died of tuberculosis when I was seven. When it came my time to go away to the war I chose the Royal Navy, just couldn't face the infantry.

I won't take you upstairs but I'll describe it to you. Up the steep stairs my room is on the left. Just a single bed and a chest of drawers to keep my clothes in. On the right is a slightly larger room which was my mother's room. She died about thirty years ago. I use this room as the guest bedroom when friends come to stay. The bathroom is out the back on the ground floor behind the kitchen. I recently had a heater put in because it gets quite cold in the winter. Apart from that it's a snug house and I'm very fond of it.

Come back into the front room and sit down. If you don't mind waiting a minute I'll make a pot of tea and bring in some scones. Some people like the jam on the cream and some the other way round. You'll be able to choose. If you wonder what I'm up to you can see into the kitchen from the back window of the room. Borrowed light they call it. Please feel free to look at any of my books. I won't be long …

… that just about concludes it. Yes, I have a lot of visitors. Some of my favourites are the local kids who come in for a chat from time to time. Sometimes I read them a poem, not always one of mine, but something suitable.

I like the idea of the University cataloguing my books one day. I don't know who will write my biography. Very dull I should think it will be. No scandal or goings on, more's the pity. It's the poetry that's important, not the tiny details of my life.

I suppose the time will come when I must go and live in a home. It will have its advantages and I'll still be here in Launceston. I've had a very good life and am very grateful for how it has turned out. I do regret not marrying and having no children or grand-children and I do feel bad that my father died so young. War is the very worst thing that can happen to mankind.

You have to go? I'll see you out. It's getting a little dimpsey so I'll put on the outside light. Out you go Rupert; but leave the rats alone. Some people were horrified when I had the lantern put up. 'Street lighting on Ridgegrove Hill?' they said. It helps those who live further down on a dark night and it certainly helps me to find the keyhole when I come home from evensong in the winter.

Good night, thanks for calling in. Have a safe journey home."

(Originally published in *An Baner Kernewek*.)

BIBLIOGRAPHY

This bibliography contains the works consulted for the biography. It is not exhaustive.

By Charles Causley:

Runaway (play). London: Curwen, 1936.

The Conquering Hero (play). London: Curwen, 1937; New York: Schirmer, 1937.

Benedict (play). London: Muller, 1938.

How Pleasant to Know Mrs Lear (play). London: Muller, 1948.

Farewell, Aggie Weston! (poems). Aldington, Kent: Hand and Flower Press, 1951.

Hands to Dance (short stories). London: Carroll and Nicholson, 1951.

Hands to Dance and Skylark (short stories with an introduction and autobiographical afterword). London: Robson, 1979.

Survivor's Leave (poems). Aldington, Kent: Hand and Flower Press, 1953.

Union Street (poems). London: Hart-Davis, 1957; Boston: Houghton Mifflin, 1958.

Johnnie Alleluia (poems). London: Hart-Davis, 1961.

Underneath the Water (poems). London: Hart-Davis, 1968.

Figure of 8 (poems). London: Macmillan, 1969.

Figgie Hobbin (children's poems). London: Macmillan, 1971; New York: Walker, 1973.

The Tail of the Trinosaur (story in verse). Leicester: Brockhampton Press, 1973.

Collected Poems 1951 – 1975. London: Macmillan, 1975; Boston: Godine, 1975.

The Hill of the Fairy Calf (story in verse). London: Hodder and Stoughton, 1976.

The Gift of a Lamb (verse play). London: Robson, 1978.
Three Heads Made of Gold (story). London: Robson, 1978.
The Last King of Cornwall (story). London: Hodder and Stoughton, 1978.
The Animals' Carol (poem). London: Macmillan, 1978.
The Ballad of Aucassin and Nicolette (play). London: Kestrel, 1981.
Secret Destinations (poems). London: Macmillan, 1984.
Twenty-One Poems (limited edition). Shipton-on-Stour, Warwickshire: Celandine Press, 1986.
Quack! Said the Billy Goat (children's poem). London: Walker Books, 1986; New York: Harper, 1986.
Early in the Morning (poems). London: Viking Kestrel, 1986.
Jack the Treacle Eater (poems). London: Macmillan, 1987.
A Field of Vision (poems). London: Macmillan, 1988.
The Young Man of Cury (poems). London: Macmillan, 1991.
All Day Saturday (poems). London: Macmillan, 1994.
Going to the Fair (poems). London: Viking, 1994.
Collected Poems for Children. London: Macmillan, 1996.
Collected Poems 1951 – 1997. London: Macmillan, 1997.
Collected Poems 1951 – 2000. London: Macmillan, 2000.
I Had a Little Cat (children's poems). London: Macmillan, 2009.

Other books consulted:

Baring-Gould, Sabine, *The Vicar of Morwenstow.* London: Methuen, 1921.
Cameron, Alick, *Charles Causley's Trusham Relatives.* Trusham: privately published.
Chambers, Harry (ed.) *Causley at 70.* Calstock: Peterloo Poets, 1987.
Hanke, Michael (ed.) *Through the Granite Kingdom: Critical Essays on Charles Causley.* Trier: Wissenschaftlicher Verlag Trier, 2011.
Kent, Alan M., *The Theatre of Cornwall.* Bristol: Westcliff Books, 2010.
Kent, Alan M., *The Theatre Works of Charles Causley.* London: Francis Boutle, 2013.
Williams, Michael, *Both Sides of the Tamar.* Bodmin: Bossiney Books, 1975.
Wright, Malcolm, *Charles Causley: A Universal Poet.* Launceston: Lawrence House Museum, 2013.
and:
Causley, Jim, *Cyprus Well.* Folk Police Recordings, 2013. With an introduction by Malcolm Wright.

ALSO BY LAURENCE GREEN

Westcountry Stories of the Restless Dead. Brixham: Moorhen, 2008.

A Hollow Sea: Thomas Prockter Ching and the Barque 'Charles Eaton'. Brixham: Moorhen, 2009.

The Way We Were (with Alice Oswald). Self published, 2010.

From Great War to Great Escape: the Two Wars of Fl. Lieut. Bernard 'Pop' Green MC. Stotfold: Fighting High, 2011.

No Admittance after Dark. Brixham: Moorhen, 2012.

Laurence Green was born on 23rd February 1950 and has lived in the same small village in south Devon since the age of six, with periods in France and California for good behaviour. He worked as a secondary school teacher for thirty years, twenty six of which were at his old school in Totnes. During this time he seemed to succeed best at frightening people or making them laugh.

A few years ago, after ten eventful years working as a wood machinist, supply teacher, classroom assistant and gardener he retired to write ghost stories and biographies. In 2004 he gained his MA in Anglo-American Literary Studies from the University of Exeter. Soon after that he started to write.

His wife Kathi and he have been happily married for forty years and have three sons. They travel a lot. At home in Devon he writes articles for magazines mainly in Cornwall, including the Cornish periodical *An Baner Kernewek*. Laurence has produced two collections of ghost stories and has also written the biography of his grandfather, Bernard 'Pop' Green, who served in both World Wars and participated in The Great Escape from Stalag Luft III.

He enjoys gardening and church affairs. He is a parish councillor and loves to visit old churches, some of which are very creepy indeed. Among the unusual things that have happened to him are: car crashes in Mexico and France, earthquakes in California and a black widow bite in the same dangerous state.

Printed in Great Britain
by Amazon